# The Way Forward
## Solutions to England's Football Failings

by Matthew Whitehouse

Published by Bennion Kearny Limited
6 Victory House
64 Trafalgar Road
Birmingham
B13 8BU

www.BennionKearny.com

Cover image: ©Shutterstock/Tigger11th

To my parents who have given me so much support
and love throughout my life.

Jade, whose patience and care has been truly wonderful.

And to Keith Harrison, who lit the flame of coaching in me
and who has been an inspiration ever since.

# Acknowledgements

The book has been a great journey for me and I have learnt much from the support and guidance of some great coaches and authors. Many coaches have asked to remain anonymous yet their insight and stories have been key to the development and depth of this book. Special mention must go to Chris Green whose help and guidance has been very much appreciated throughout.

Without doubt the most important help for me has been the support of my publisher – Bennion Kearny. Without them, this book would not have been possible and I appreciate the assistance of all those people who saw value in this project, and who trusted me to make it possible.

# About the Author

Matthew Whitehouse is a professional football coach who has worked across the globe. A UEFA 'A' licenced coach with a Master's degree in Sports Coaching he has extensive experience both academically and practically on coaching and youth development.

Matthew is also a prominent and influential writer and is the editor of the award winning *The Whitehouse Address* blog.

# Table of Contents

# Part I

# England's Past Failures

# 1

# The End of the
# Golden Generation

*"I've been brought up over the last few years believing this was the golden generation. If this is the golden generation, the sooner we move away from the gold standard the better."*
Lord Mawhinney, Ex-Football League chairman in the wake of England's failure to reach the 2008 European championships.

## Crisis, what crisis?

It has been quite a decade for English football. Not since the late 1970's and early 1980's when Liverpool, Nottingham Forest and Aston Villa were lifting the European Cup six years in a row have English clubs been so dominant in Europe's top competition. Between 2005 and 2012 there was an English side represented in the Champions League final all but once. Of those seven finals an English side lifted the trophy three times.

During those years it appeared that Premier League sides were simply overpowering 'foreign' sides. The strength and intensity of the English game was too much for many across Europe. This 'dominance' gave the English media and fans a belief that they were superior to the rest and led the media to portray the English league as the best.

Unfortunately, over the past few seasons, English clubs' dominance has started to wane. The modern game has evolved and with it the Premier League has lost its superiority across Europe. The truth is that the power and strength which made English clubs such a force has been replaced by a more technical and tactical game across the continent.

# A decade of dominance comes to an end

While English sides were lifting European cups, our media was attempting to make this out to be a success for England. The truth is slightly different. Yes, Liverpool, Arsenal, Manchester United and Chelsea are all English clubs, yet none of them were managed by an English coach when they were lifting trophies Furthermore, their teams were made up with more foreign players than English ones.

In the final against Milan in 2005 Liverpool had only two Englishmen in the side: Steven Gerrard and Jamie Carragher. In 2006 Arsenal played Barcelona and they too only had two English players in their side: Ashley Cole and Sol Campbell. 2007 saw Liverpool and Milan face off again, this time Jermaine Pennant joined Gerrard and Carragher.

2008 saw an all English final between Manchester United and Chelsea. Whether impressive or not - 10 of the 22 outfield players were English: Wes Brown, Rio Ferdinand, Owen Hargreaves, Paul Scholes, Michael Carrick, and Wayne Rooney played for United. Chelsea had John Terry, Ashley Cole, Frank Lampard and Joe Cole. It was the core of the England national team.

> Over the last decade, the Premier League's success has been built on foreign coaches and players, not English ones.

The following season would see a significant change in European football. Manchester United had reached the final for the second consecutive time and were on course to rival Arrigo Sacchi's AC Milan to win back-to-back European cups. However in their place was Pep Guardiola's Barcelona – a team on course to win an unprecedented treble.

Spain had won the European Championships the summer before; the tournament England had failed to qualify for. Although Barcelona had won the Champions League in 2006, there was something special about this particular group of players. Barcelona would win the 2009 final 2-0 with goals from Samuel Eto'o and Lionel Messi.

Yet it was the Spanish spine of Valdes, Puyol, Pique, Busquets, Xavi and Iniesta who would dictate the game and who would show the world a new style of playing the game. That final was a strong indication that English football's dominance in Europe was over.

Two years later the two sides would meet again and this time, fittingly, at England's 'home', Wembley. Ferguson had promised he had learned from his errors the time before, yet this would be an even more one-sided demolition of England's champions.

Barcelona were simply mesmerising; their movement, technical ability, vision and intensity were too much for a tired and weary looking United side which ultimately lost 3-1. Barcelona's technicians and the side's tactical acumen were too much for United's functional 4-5-1 formation. It was symbolic: United's performance encapsulated English football's decline.

Of course, Chelsea were to lift the trophy in 2012, yet the manner in which they won was again significant. The vast wealth of Roman Abramovich had assembled a strong and physical side, yet throughout their journey to the final it was a side which had needed to hang on with near desperation at times.

It was a perfect metaphor of how English football itself had been clinging on desperately to a previous decade while European football was evolving and modernising its approach, leaving England very much behind.

# The Golden Generation

The Premier League's 'success' had confused and tricked many into believing that because English club teams have performed well, historically, in European competition, then the national team was also strong. However, since the league's inception in 1993, the English national team has only gone beyond the quarter-finals of a major tournament once, on home-soil, in 1996.

For over a decade we have been told by our media that the English league is the best in the world. That we possess the best players, coaches, fans and provide the most entertainment. They tell us – the Premier League is how football should be played. Pundits, former stars, and respected journalists start selling a triumphant national team before each tournament.

For decades England has entered tournament after tournament with the hopes and dreams of their nation on its shoulders, and returned as 'failures'. Each tournament is supposed to be 'the one'. The one where it all clicks together and our world class stars perform to the level that they do - week in week out - in the Premier League. Each time they are expected to win and come back home victorious, yet each time it ends in tears.

For the past decade, England fans have been led to believe that English football was blessed with a 'Golden Generation' of talent which could rival any team in world football. It turns out this was a fallacy.

The 'Golden Generation' was a phrase coined by the ex-chief executive of the English FA, Adam Crozier, in 2002. It was said early into the reign of Sven-Goran Eriksson and perhaps meant as a motivational tool. However it would be a phrase which the English media would use for the following decade to punish England's constant 'failures'.

Finally, after a decade of disappointment, we have realised that in terms of being top players in the international game the Golden Generation was never as great as we were led to believe.

However to point blame at this Golden Generation solely would suggest that English sides before them had achieved something of note. It has been almost 50 years since England lifted the World Cup in 1966 and in that time very little progress has truly been made.

After the World Cup in 1966 English football never pushed on to become a major competitor in international football. In fact, as each decade passed England appeared further away from recapturing that World Cup. Each international tournament since has brought only agony and disappointment.

The reasons why England fail are discussed vehemently after each tournament; fingers are pointed and questions are asked. Yet those questions are never answered satisfactorily. The national side has continuously failed and few lessons appear to be learned.

> Coaches, players and the FA have been guilty of doing the same things each time and expecting different results.

# November 2007 - a valuable wakeup call?

The failure to reach the 2008 European Championships appeared to represent the necessary 'wake-up call' for English football as the qualifying campaign highlighted the issues plaguing the national team. A lack of technical ability and 'skill' was evident when compared to the Croatians in the team's fatal November 2007 defeat.

The Croatian side (from a country with a population of roughly 4 million) possessed skill, confidence, cohesion and tactical understanding. They outclassed an England side that played with little self-belief, confidence or understanding. A decade after Howard Wilkinson had laid down his Charter for Quality England appeared more of a shambles than Graham Taylor's side which failed to qualify in 1994.

The similarities to the humiliating defeat to Hungary in 1953 were not lost on many after the defeat to Croatia. Another November night, some 55 years earlier, saw Hungary win 6-3 at Wembley and embarrass an England side which had never been beaten on home soil before. Puskas and his compatriots simply played football from another world. They had taken the game which England had created and made it so much better. A feat that many other nations have done since.

England's coach, Steve McClaren, was made to look foolish by the Croatian coach Slaven Bilic. McClaren was apparently the best coach England has produced recently, yet he had no answers or solutions to Croatia. That night Croatia had so much space and time and they punished a woeful England. Quite simply they were a team equipped for modern football, whereas England was a side very much behind the times.

> The failure to plan for the long term
> has been England's failing.

The loss eliminated England from the tournament and sealed the fate of McClaren. Excuses were made, such as the absence of both Wayne Rooney and the preferred defence, yet this issue highlighted further the problems regarding depth of quality in a nation of 60 million people.

After the game Croatia's coach Slaven Bilic was ruthless in his comments. "I read in the papers not one Croatian player would get in the England team. I strongly advise you to wake up."

## Failure to learn once again?

After this failure England went abroad to improve matters. The esteemed Italian coach Fabio Capello was brought in to turn the Golden Generation into winners. In fact, he was brought in not just to succeed with the senior side but also to revolutionise the whole structure of the game.

The FA wanted Capello to lay down a blueprint for England's future. Yet by all accounts he didn't do anything of the sort. Many will tell you that he did very little except PR events. And even with the senior side he presided over the same players who had fallen short before.

Capello did take England to the World Cup in 2010 yet, at the tournament, England were abject against the USA and Algeria (who outplayed England throughout) and a dismal exit to an exciting and fresh German team produced vicious condemnation from fans and the media. The Germans looked built for modern football whereas England looked a shambles.

The truth was that England was not good enough to succeed. Previously, the FA had believed that it was the coach who was failing the players and brought in foreign managers. They were wrong. They believed England had a side which was capable of winning tournaments. They were wrong again. Sven-Goran Eriksson and Fabio Capello failed to succeed in the same way as Kevin Keegan before them.

Roy Hodgson's appointment as England manager was met with mixed feelings yet, in his time with England, he has shown how he sees the need to evolve the England side. Yes England were knocked out of Euro 2012 at the quarter final stage (on penalties once again) and performances were functional at best yet Hodgson appears to understand the failings of the past decade and knows the amount of work needed to make the England national team a competitive force.

England's performances have stemmed from a failure to plan for the long term. Each tournament has been built up to be the one where success is destined to come; where all the past planning and development miraculously (and finally) 'comes together'. This viewpoint has meant that the team has failed to evolve; young players have not been developed sufficiently and while other nations have advanced, England has effectively stood still.

## Summary

After the Golden Generation we have been left with a new generation that lacks the necessary qualities and experience needed for top level football. As this book will make clear, English football has been left behind. Yet it is not just the group of players which is to blame. Important changes in youth development, coaching and culture are necessary for the future success of the English game.

Without necessary change there will be no improvement. To prepare for the future, you must learn from the past and as the following chapters will examine, the key for England's future is to learn from the terrible mistakes and decisions from the previous decades.

# 2

# The World's Greatest League

*"It's an English club but not an English success; it's probably a greater reflection of youngsters from France and elsewhere in Europe. It's hard to say that it speaks volumes for English football when none of the players is home grown."*
Graham Taylor speaking about Arsenal in March 2006 after they defeated Real Madrid in the Champions League, without a single English player in their team.

## The Premier League has created a fallacy

In 1993 the Premier League was born. It was formed to take advantage of a lucrative television deal that would see top English teams break away from the Football League.

Through the increasing popularity of the league in England and abroad, Premier League revenues from television have risen astronomically providing English clubs in the top league with vast wealth. The current television deal is worth a staggering £5.5 billion over a three year period, starting with the 2013/14 season. The Premier League has become a commercial goldmine and the clubs, players, and their agents have benefited grandly from it.

With the money in the game today, and the potential riches of the Premier League and Champions League, English football has become a delightful prospect for foreign businessmen and players. The appeal of owning a Premier League club has therefore become seen as either an 'investment' or an expensive 'hobby' for some owners. Either way the expectations on a club's management is simple: stay in the league and be successful.

English football has welcomed foreign investment to soak up debts, and the hope of propelling clubs into the elite of world football. For some clubs foreign ownership and investment has helped, but it has also affected the future of others as well as reducing the quality of players and coaches of English heritage.

In turn, the past decade has seen a worrying trend emerge in England's top league. An overreliance on foreign talent has materialized, the justification being that the top teams need to import top talent in order to challenge and maintain their status in the 'world's greatest league'.

> The Premier League has had a negative effect on the development of English players and the success of the England national team.

## A lack of opportunity for home grown talent?

As the league has excelled and prospered, the dearth of home grown talent has become ever more apparent. Sponsors and advertisers demand immediate results to appease shareholders, therefore the established player has become preferred over young talent. As Jim Cassell, the former Manchester City academy director, said in an interview in *The Daily Telegraph,* "There is so much pressure at the top, managers want instant results. They don't have time to work on the players and grow them."

The English Premier League has become so international, and so success driven, that it seems difficult to produce domestic players through the top teams. The statistics are very concerning: only 38% of players in the league are English. For all the advantages that foreign players and coaches have brought to the English game, the truth is we have a league filled with more than 60% foreign players.

The diminution of opportunities for young English players is an increasingly worrying threat. A report by the Professional Footballers' Association (PFA) in 2007, entitled *Meltdown,* stated that, "The number of overseas players making Premier League debuts every season is running at three times that of English players coming into the game through the Academy system." It appears self-evident that these foreign players are restricting the development of home grown English talent due to the high demands of immediate success.

And it is not just players. Did you know that an English manager has never won the Premier League? The last English manager to win the top division was Howard Wilkinson with Leeds in 1992, the season before the Premier League began. In turn, the last time an English coach won a European trophy was in 1985, when Howard Kendall won the Cup Winners' Cup with Everton.

> Foreign talent is valued more highly than domestic talent.
> There needs to be serious questions asked as to why.

## The club versus country argument

Do top clubs like Arsenal, Chelsea and Manchester City really want to develop young English talent or is recruiting the *best players* (irrespective of nationality) their key focus? Subsequently, the club over country argument arises again.

Due to the league structure in England a club is not at the behest of the Football Association and therefore does not buy or train players for the benefit of the national side. The clubs believe that they have no obligation to supply players for the national team; instead they seek to bring in the best players to make their team successful.

Club managers are given a remit to win games. Thus, the justification for not developing youth players is simple. Managers cannot take risks on young players that could affect results and ultimately their jobs. Managers choose to bring in more experienced players who can help the team bring positive results. And many fans are content with their team succeeding, no matter the odds and whatever the nationality of their team's players. It is only when England are knocked out in tournaments do we hear the concerns.

Based on the *Meltdown* report and concerns surrounding sides like Arsenal, in particular, for fielding all-foreign teams - the PFA backed UEFA proposals for each club's squad to contain eight home grown players. This was initially agreed in 2006 yet it would take four years until the rule was implemented. The failure to qualify for the 2008 European Championships may have been the catalyst which English football needed to push the rule through.

In 2010/11 the 'home grown' rule was introduced by the Premier League in order to address the lack of English talent playing in England's top league. Premier League clubs were restricted to naming a squad of 25 players, eight of which were required to be 'home grown'. It appeared a positive step for the development and integration of more English players. And yet, the term 'home grown' became ambiguous and failed to address the problem it sought to fix. In fact it may have made the situation worse for English football.

The definition of home grown is "Trained for three years under the age of 21 by somebody in the English and Welsh professional system." Thus a Spanish player like Cesc Fabregas (for instance) *would* have been deemed home grown as he arrived at Arsenal at 17 years of age, and then trained for three years. In fact, with this rule, clubs have sought to bring in foreign players at even younger ages in order to make them eligible as 'home grown'. Many would argue, therefore, that the rule has actually hampered the development of English players.

# A matter of quality

As mentioned above, the number of English players playing in the Premier League is 38%, compared to Italy, Germany and Spain which have more than 60% domestic players playing in their top leagues. Clearly England is far behind these national teams and the implication is that the national side has been sacrificed for the benefit and riches of club football.

It is clear that Premier League clubs, as well as the Premier League itself, do not care about the national team. Success comes first and if that means foreign players who are better than English ones then so be it. The clubs want to stay in the richest league in the world and sponsors want to ensure the best talent is in the league in order to retain the entertainment and quality needed to make billions of pounds for those involved.

The issue therefore is *why* foreign players are seen as better options than English ones. Managers in English clubs will argue that the majority of English players are simply 'not good enough' for the top levels of the game, when compared to other players from abroad. On top of this has risen the 'premium' of buying English.

For the majority of clubs in the Premier League - signing mediocre, average English players for disproportionately high fees and wages is not deemed to be good business. Foreign players are of better quality in terms of technical and tactical ability, yet cost less also.

In recent seasons Newcastle United has invested in foreign talent, predominantly from France and Holland. Players like Cheik Tiote, Yohann Cabaye and Hatem Ben Arfa have all arrived for several million pounds and have made a big impact. The policy has been low risk and high gain both financially and on the pitch.

Contrast this to Liverpool which has invested huge sums into English players such as Andy Carroll, Stewart Downing, Jordan Henderson and Daniel Sturridge (they cost a combined £90 million). These players are clearly not worth the scale of money paid for them in fees or wages and Liverpool have, in contrast to Newcastle, suffered both on the pitch *and* financially.

Some major questions arise from this situation. Firstly, why are English players so expensive? It seems rather ludicrous that players who are seen as 'average' in comparison to other players from around the world are worth so much. The answer may simply be that restricted supply inflates their worth. It appears that as fewer English players of quality are being developed, a higher premium has been put on those who do play in the league. Many are overhyped by the media and agents because they are 'English'. Accordingly, we witness an over-inflation of English talent that does not reflect reality.

Based on this, the problem for the England national team has been that many top sides find it much more financially prudent to buy cheaper foreign talent than pay over the odds for an Englishman who is of the same quality. This means that a limited number of English players are exposed to football of the highest level, which impacts upon the size of the talent pool for the national side.

Would a national manager want to field a team with players who *have not* been exposed to top Premier League and European football? Probably not. Yet this is becoming the situation for the England manager.

The purchasing and development patterns of the top teams are affecting the England national team because of a lack of opportunity to 'bring on' players which leads to a lack of competition for places.

> It makes more financial sense to purchase players from abroad than buy home grown talent.

## Why do clubs feel the need to recruit talent from abroad?

The reason clubs are buying foreign talent is that we are not creating players of the necessary quality for the league. Foreign players are not only financially more viable yet they seem to have better skills and ability than many English players.

This is having a detrimental effect on the development of top quality English players, as there are not enough going to top teams to improve further, because they are simply too expensive. Newcastle and Arsenal have shown that bringing in foreign players for lower costs not only helps the side on the pitch yet also improves the finances of the side when those players are sold on.

So the argument shifts to why clubs are not developing their own English players? Surely the 'raw player material' should be broadly similar across countries? And should not English players cost less to develop than an imported player, and be worth more when fully developed? These questions are the fundamental focus of this book. Surely by developing our own players teams would reduce costs as it is much cheaper to develop talent, and doing so would improve the national team too?

The mentality across many academies across England is that English players are not good enough compared to foreign players of the same age. They do not feel inclined to accept the mediocre levels of English talent when they can afford to bring in better talent from abroad. Fulham's U18 side recently fielded a side with no English players and Manchester City is stockpiling foreign players for their youth sides also.

Because of the riches in the Premier League, clubs are not particularly restricted and for them quality is key, not nationality. For as long as there are no rules limiting how many foreign players *play* for a team, clubs will seek to recruit the best talent around.

It follows that the fundamental issue is: if English players aren't amongst the best – *why not?*

## Summary

The quality of English players hasn't necessarily deteriorated in recent years, in fact it can be argued to have improved. Yet the standard they have to reach has become much higher. It is now necessary to be world class in order to compete with the global talent in world football.

In the following chapters, we will look at why failed philosophies and ideals have hampered the future generations of English football and put the English team (as well as its players) so far behind the rest.

# 3

# A Failed Vision which Ruined a Nation's Future

*"I want to establish without any shadow of a doubt that Charles Hughes is totally wrong in his approach to football."*
Two time European Cup winner Brian Clough.

## The English stereotype

England's captain in 1966, Bobby Moore, was admired for his great positioning, perfectly timed tackles and superb ability to read the game. He was also universally respected for his leadership and reputation as a true gentleman. He was the greatest defender Pelé ever played against.

It would make logical sense that Bobby Moore should have been the model on which English football prided itself and developed its future players. Yet decades later the English player was stereotyped as brave, aggressive and courageous, more a soldier than a footballer.

English football became personified by Terry Butcher's blood stained shirt in 1989 and Stuart Pearce's famous 'celebration' after a penalty against Spain in 1996. So much passion, dedication, and desire.

These images highlighted where English football had gone. This evolution of the country's mentality is one reason why England has not been to a major final since their success of 1966.

How did English football get to this stage? Well, they say 'football is a game of opinions' and that is undeniably true - yet when one man's opinion about how to play the game was implemented, a country was laid in ruin. The results were seen for decades to come and English football has still not fully recovered.

## How the FA ruined the English game

In the 1950s Wolverhampton Wanderers were one of the best sides in Europe. Led by their iconic manger Stan Cullis (who would take the club on the most successful period in their history) Wolverhampton would win the league three times and the FA cup twice during the 1950's and early 1960's.

Stan Cullis had particular views on how football should be played, views which became very influential and which laid the foundations for the development of the English game. Cullis wanted the ball in front of the opposition goal as much, and as quickly, as possible. He did not want his defenders to spend too long on the ball and particularly not have the ball in his team's half for very long because if they lost the ball - the opposition could score. Effectively, get the ball forward as soon as possible, and score more goals!

The above could be the shortened version of the FA's coaching manual for the 50 years that followed.

In 1963, Allen Wade became the technical director of the FA. A role he stayed in until 1983. After England's World Cup win in 1966 Wade sat down to start writing *The FA Guide to Training and Coaching*, a book that, when published the following year, was to become a 'Bible' to generations of coaches.

Wades' idea was to treat football teams as an 'organic whole'. The team's shape took precedence over the individual. During his time at the FA he laid down ideas and taught coaches a style of playing and football coaching which, it might be argued, went against the common trends of that era.

While Brazil, Holland, Germany and Argentina were developing creative, skilful and expansive players, as well as teams that played excellent football 'on the floor' (and successfully so) England were being instructed to develop functional teams ahead of ones containing creative and skilful players.

> "Team shape over the individual" screams out the problems
> that England has faced as a competitive nation
> over the past few decades.

# The death of English football

When Wade left the FA, in 1983, the England national team had experienced a disappointing decade; failure to qualify for the 1974 and 1978 World Cups as well as the 1972 and 1976 European championships highlighted serious issues regarding England's ability on the international stage.

Although the 1980's would see England qualify for tournaments again, there was a concern that the England team and its players were little match for some of the world's top nations.

Following Wade's departure, his close friend Charles Hughes was appointed as the FA's new technical director. With Charles Hughes, the English FA would not only continue to promote Allen Wades' ideas and coaching methods, they would take them even further, putting the future of English football in even greater jeopardy.

Hughes authored the FA's official coaching manual and laid the footings for the future of English football. Hughes took on from Cullis and Wade a belief that direct football was the key to a team's success. In fact he became an even stronger advocate of long ball tactics, asserting in his book *The Winning Formula* that, "The strategy of direct play is far more preferable to that of possession football. The facts are irrefutable and the evidence overwhelming." Very strong and very damaging words.

His assertions went as far as to argue that world football had got it wrong; in *The Winning Formula* Hughes claimed, "World soccer has been moving in the wrong direction for the better part of thirty years."

Yes, that is right. Charles Hughes believed that sides like Germany, Brazil and Holland were playing football the 'wrong way'. That possession-based football was flawed. He believed that these sides were 'overplaying'. For Hughes, a failure to hit the ball forward as much as possible, in the fewest number of passes possible, resulted in sides reducing their chances of scoring.

Hughes believed that nations like Brazil could not teach England anything. It did not occur to Hughes to learn from the best and most successful nations of that time, instead he criticised them for playing a style which he considered 'flawed'. Incredible.

Hughes' beliefs were so mistaken as to border on delusional. And yet his ideas were to be implemented and taught to future coaches in England. The English FA were about to develop coaches who would teach and implement this style.

As you can see, the foundations and philosophy for English football were being laid down and cemented during Hughes' first years as technical director. In men like Wade and Hughes English football went against what the top nations and successful sides were doing and producing. Whether through arrogance or ignorance these men would effectively ruin future generations of English football.

> The FA would educate their coaches on a direct style of football – which would ruin the future of English football for years to come.

## A failure to learn from those lifting trophies

Interestingly, as Hughes was coming into his role at the FA, English clubs were dominating European football. From 1976-1984 English clubs won the European Cup in all but one season. Liverpool won the cup three times, Nottingham Forest twice, and Aston Villa once.

Yet Charles Hughes' style was not to be seen in these European cup winning sides. In fact, his style was to be found in lower league English sides like Watford and Wimbledon. This sentence alone highlights the problems, failings and restrictions which English football was on course to embrace.

While Liverpool and Forest espoused a possession-based passing game, Watford and Wimbledon would be playing a strand of football that went in the opposite direction. It favoured a high octane style simply referred to as 'kick and rush'. It was a playing style which was seen as brutish and anti-football. It was precisely what Hughes was seeking.

Under their manager, Graham Taylor, Watford sought to enter the final third of the pitch as quickly and as often as possible through the use of long direct balls to their forward. The intention was to get close to the opposition goal looking for knock downs or seeking to win the ball back high up the pitch.

Impressively, over the course of five years, Taylor would take Watford from the Fourth Division to Division One and Europe. It was not until his first season in Europe, when Taylor began to find opponents coming up with solutions to his direct style. After losing 7-2 on aggregate to Sparta Prague, Taylor lamented, "It was men against boys, when you gave the ball away, they didn't give it back to you."

Jonathan Wilson, in his book *Inverting the Pyramid*, summarised the situation neatly, "And there, precisely, is the problem with the direct style of play based on pressing. It's all well and good until you come up against a side good enough technically to be able to keep possession even when under pressure."

This should have been a lesson to the English FA, a lesson that Hughes' direct football was a limited style which would not improve England's national team. Instead of championing the success of Watford, Hughes should have been learning from England's genuinely successful sides at the time, Liverpool and Nottingham Forest, who were playing a style of football that was in contrast to what the English Football Association was proposing… and lifting European Cups in doing so.

> Watford was held up as an example of the
> benefits of 'direct football' yet in reality it was
> a failed philosophy at the top level.

## Liverpool learnt the only way to play

Through the Stan Cullis, Allen Wade, and Charles Hughes decades the English game was characterised by goal mouth incidents and high tempo football. The game was 'sold' as boring unless it was played at 100mph. Yet this encapsulated the problems of English sides in Europe and internationally. Liverpool learnt that this way of playing the game was not conducive for success across Europe.

During the Shankly years at Liverpool, in the infamous 'boot room', there was much discussion regarding Liverpool's vulnerabilities in Europe. Shankly had spoken of European sides being prepared to hold possession and frustrate their opponents.

Liverpool's struggles in Europe under Shankly had taught Liverpool an important lesson: As Shankly highlighted, "The Europeans showed that building from the back is the only way to play. It started in Europe and we adapted it into our game at Liverpool where our system had always been a collective one."

Shankly's aims for his side were simple. "The main aim is that everyone can control a ball and do the basic things in football. It's control and pass, control and pass, all the time." These quotes should have been a blueprint for English football, successful football even, where players are developed to be comfortable with the ball, where possession football is seen not only as aesthetically pleasing but necessary to play and succeed in Europe. Shankly learnt the errors of English football, yet Charles Hughes went completely the other way.

When Bob Paisley took over the reins at Anfield he evolved Liverpool's approach based on Shankly's beliefs. Paisley taught the English that their approach was wrong and he would take Liverpool to another level in terms of success. The mark of their improvements would be in contrast to the England national team who, at that time, were struggling to qualify for major tournaments.

> Liverpool learnt that the 'English' way was not working
> and sought to become more 'continental' in their
> style. It would prove to be very successful.

Liverpool's style would be similar to the approach that Nottingham Forest had under Brian Clough. Clough would win two European Cups playing a style of football which promoted the ball being played on the floor. It was simple and effective in its approach yet it required players who were comfortable on the ball, players who had skill and composure. It was these sides, these coaches, who should have been writing England's future. Instead English football was put in the hands of men who had no idea about football. No wonder England have failed to push on since their success in 1966.

## Summary

Direct play, as an oversimplification of the game, resulted in the stagnation and (ultimately) the failure of the England national side for decades to come. Through a flawed and misguided philosophy, English football had failed to develop players capable of competing at the top level.

As the following chapter will highlight, Charles Hughes would produce a crisis in the development of individuals capable of playing, and succeeding, in the modern game.

# 4

# English Football's
# Biggest Crime

*"When I played for England it was in a 4-4-2 and I chased the ball quite a lot in the 1980s - that's why I've never really played the formation as a manager at international level."*
Glenn Hoddle.

## How Michels taught the English their error

Whilst at the English FA, Allen Wade believed that team shape and organisation was greater than 'individual quality'. In respects to valuing shape and teamwork he was right, success in football is often built on teamwork and being a complete 'team'. Yet he got it horribly wrong when it came to the needs of the individual player. He saw the ideas of compactness and organisation more akin to 'trench warfare' and he saw skill or anything which resembled creativity as a danger to that organised 'whole'.

While English football's teachers were nullifying the individual, and neglecting skill over functionality, nations such as Holland were developing teams with similar ideas of 'the whole' yet producing players who could play skilful attacking football.

Rinus Michels was a Dutch footballer who became one of the most successful and pioneering coaches in football history. After finishing his playing career he took over as manager of Ajax in 1965 and, with players such as Johan Cruyff and Johan Neeskens, would take them from relegation candidates to a team that would win the league championship four times between 1966 and 1970. His greatest achievement would be to win the European Cup in 1971 defeating Panathinaikos in the final. That success would be followed by two more successive European Cup successes which would make that Ajax side one of the best in football history.

Michels would be appointed as Dutch national team coach in 1974. Playing with the style which had brought Ajax so much success, Michels would take the team to the 1974 World Cup final only to be defeated by West Germany 2-1. A true compliment to the quality of that side and the performances they produced has meant that when people talk about the 1974 World Cup they talk only of Holland and forget who actually won the tournament.

Michels with his *totaalvoetbal* ('total football') would use the famed 4-3-3 formation, seeking to dominate and control games with attacking football. His logic during the 1960's and 1970's was very different to the English mentality at that time. In England the players were almost fixed in their positions yet under Michels his players were not stuck to one position; for him freedom and the interchanging of positions was the key to successful football.

Michels made sure each player knew the roles and responsibilities of each position and if a player on the pitch moved out of his position, another player would fill the hole. The team would *keep its shape* while allowing its players to roam and be creative. It was total football.

Johan Cruyff was the jewel of Dutch football and was the key man behind the success of Ajax under Michels. His skill, craft and vision made him one of the world's best playmakers. In the late 1980's Cruyff would become the manager of Barcelona and would lay down the style of play he learnt under Michels. He would put together the famous 'Dream Team' which saw flowing and beautiful football. As well as that he would make sure that the Barcelona academy would develop players in the Dutch method.

Cruyff laid the foundations of total football at Barcelona which would produce world class players such as Xavi Hernandez, Andres Iniesta and Lionel Messi. Success has been forthcoming both for Barcelona and Spain who in the past decade have won three Champions Leagues, two European Championships, and a World Cup. Total football has lived on and proved very successful in the modern game.

Since the time of Cruyff, Holland has produced some really talented players in the form of the De Boer twins, Ronald Koeman, Edgar Davids, Clarence Seedorf, Marco van Basten, Ruud Gullit, Frank Rijkaard and Dennis Bergkamp to name but a few. The recurring theme of all these players is that they had complete confidence on the ball, possessing vision, creativity and skill.

For a nation of roughly six million Holland has produced some exceptional talents. Through Michels' philosophy, the nation has taught the world how to develop exceptional talent which can now be seen in the success of Spain and Barcelona.

One can only look on with a sense of jealousy to see what Spain and Barcelona have done in recent years to underscore the influence and value of Michels, Cruyff and the Dutch model of youth development.

> It is clear that it is not about a country's size –
> it is about their philosophies.

# A revolutionary who never played the game

There was another man, an Italian who would be inspired by Michels' teams and methods. He was not an ex-footballer yet was a passionate and intelligent coach and his 4-4-2 would bring a Serie A title and two back-to-back European Cups in 1989 and 1990 for AC Milan.

Arrigo Sacchi made great strides in his coaching career at an early age and moved to Fiorentina to work with their youth team. His achievements there would gain interest from Parma who were, at that time, playing in Serie C1. He would get Parma promoted to Serie B in his first season and, over the following season, would take them to within three points of promotion to Serie A. During his time at Parma, Sacchi would face AC Milan where he would defeat the Rossoneri 1-0. Parma's performance in that game alerted Milan's owner to Sacchi and he would appoint him as Milan manager in 1987.

The press were quick to dismiss Sacchi and his lack of experience, professing that such an inadequate player could never go on to be a successful coach. This is when Sacchi coined his famous phrase, "A jockey doesn't have to have been born a horse."

There was no surprise that Sacchi, who was an admirer of Michels' philosophy, brought in three attacking Dutch players because they had been developed in the style of Michels' 'Total Football'. Ruud Gullit, Marco van Basten and Frank Rijkaard would provide the creative attacking impetus which provided moments of true brilliance.

As well as the Dutch trio, Milan possessed defenders who could pass the football. In Franco Baresi, Paolo Maldini and Roberto Donadoni - Sacchi had the necessary players and quality to play the football he wanted. They had composure on the ball and were capable of finding teammates with accurate and precise passes. The importance of having ball playing defenders was key for the coaches who played total football. If their defenders could not pass effectively then the style would not work.

Sacchi's training methods and style of play proved to be hugely successful. His Milan side was near perfect in terms of pressing, compactness, and counter attacking. One could argue that they resembled an Allen Wade team yet the difference was fluidity, genuine skill, and creativity in the side.

Although Sacchi played a 4-4-2 formation Milan did not resemble England when in possession, it was nothing like the 'kick and rush' football of the English game. Milan was a whole organism working together, playing with class and style. For Sacchi's style to work it was important that he allowed fluidity and the interchange of roles and positions. As well as this he made sure his team had genuine individual quality.

The examples of Michels, Cruyff and Sacchi highlight the problem that English football faced. Coaches in England were instructed to be organised and compact yet - fatally - any regard for skill or technical quality was dismissed. Defenders were instructed to merely 'lump' the ball forward in the hope that the tall powerful striker could do something with it.

## A proponent of the FA's methods

There is no doubting that English football suffered because of the direct, safety first mentality. Players were developed by coaches indoctrinated in the English FA methods. The style of the English game was (and remains) the reason for the country's failings on the international stage and in the development of world class players.

In 1990, the FA chose Graham Taylor as the national team's manager. As discussed earlier Taylor was a major proponent of direct football, and English football suffered greatly. The previous manager, Bobby Robson, had taken England to a penalty shootout away from the 1990 World Cup final, with players such as Peter Beardsley, Paul Gascoigne, John Barnes and Chris Waddle. But Taylor would take the team backwards.

At the 1992 European Championships Taylor would dismiss the creative players used under Robson and choose more 'functional' players such as Tony Daley, Carlton Palmer and Andy Sinton in the attacking positions. England would finish bottom of their group and would subsequently fail to qualify for the 1994 World Cup.

Under a manager who valued 'functional' players over skill and creativity English football was in crisis. Taylor, the epitome of the English FA's doctrine and beliefs, would prove what a failure it was.

After Taylor, some promising signs emerged that England was finally becoming more adaptable in their approach, style and formation. Terry Venables would show some innovation in his time as England manager and with his 'Christmas tree' formation of 4-3-2-1 took England to the semi-final at the 1996 European Championships, and another penalty shootout defeat. Venables was succeeded by Glenn Hoddle, who was more than aware of England's failing formation and style of play. He had been a player who had suffered personally from its rigidity and limitations. The quote at the start of the chapter illustrates his viewpoint.

Hoddle was the youngest England manager in history and after being aware of the constraints and drawbacks of the past decades he sought to change England's style. In an article written for the *Daily Mail*, Hoddle discussed his wish to 'modernise' the English game, "I was trying to change the English way of playing, after 10 years of personally chasing shadows in midfield, where we were outnumbered, I wanted to play 3-5-2, giving us three in midfield and still two in attack."

A 3-5-2 formation was almost revolutionary for English football and perhaps it could have been successful had England not gone down to 10 men (following the sending off of David Beckham) against Argentina in the 1998 World Cup. Even with a player less England got to those dreaded penalties once again, and lost, again.

Unfortunately for English football Hoddle would damage his reputation with his interview in *The Times* in the January of 1999, an interview where he would attempt to defend his religious beliefs. In an interview with Matt Dickinson, Hoddle revealed his controversial belief that the disabled and others are being punished for sins in a former life. It led to much criticism from politicians and the media campaign against him was extreme. A poll by the BBC found that 90% of respondents believed Hoddle should not continue as England manager. Hoddle refused to quit yet with his position as England manager effectively untenable the FA sacked him in February 1999.

For English football it was disappointing because in Hoddle England had shown progression and change towards the modern game. An overloaded midfield with players such as Paul Scholes in the team to control and dictate the game had given the team a new dimension to the rigid and functional 4-4-2.

After Hoddle, England would return to their mediocre style. Kevin Keegan would oversee a horrible European Championship in 2000 having reverted back to the functional 4-4-2. England returned to being overloaded in midfield by sides like Portugal and Romania. David Beckham and Steve McManaman, who both had more ability than being just orthodox 'wingers', were restricted in their wide roles and Paul Scholes and Paul Ince were overrun in midfield. A strike-force of Shearer and Owen were isolated because of the return to the formation which Hoddle professed made you 'chase shadows'.

# The Golden Generation's restrictions

The English 4-4-2 is a system which does not account for changes in the modern game or, equally importantly, which does not allow top players to fit into the team. It is therefore no surprise that when England have encountered a good side, they have ultimately lost.

Proponents of the 4-4-2 formation will highlight its simplicity and how 'tough and resilient' it can be. Yet it is a more defensive style of play, which appears to admit that England are inferior to other nations. As Jonathan Wilson argues, "It is not a formation which will produce thrilling or proactive football." Not exactly the type of style which you want to build your youth development on. Yet this is what has happened for the past several decades.

> One can only imagine how a little tactical ingenuity
> could have made England a better side.

In the early years of the 2000's the 4-4-2 approach became redundant for England's top sides. It was not being used by Manchester United, Liverpool, Arsenal or Chelsea. Under their foreign coaches they were playing a more European style of football in a 4-2-3-1 or 4-3-3 formation. As Hoddle had stated - a three man midfield was deemed necessary to control games and win matches.

Arsenal were playing a very fluid 4-4-2 which really was seen as a 4-2-3-1 with two holding midfielders, Bergkamp in the 10 role, and two fast wingers supplying Thierry Henry. And when Rafa Benitez arrived at Liverpool, he used the style which had brought Valencia such success. It was this style which would see the club reach two Champions League finals. And under Mourinho Chelsea would play a 4-3-3 which was easily converted to a 4-2-3-1.

Thus, England's top sides, none of them managed by an English coach, were playing a style more conducive to the modern game. The irony became that playing for England was 'foreign' for these players.

For England there was the constant dilemma for each manager of how to fit players such as Paul Scholes, David Beckham Joe Cole, Frank Lampard and Steven Gerrard into the 4-4-2. This problem caused England many problems in terms of both balance and effectiveness. Yet, amazingly, there was never a consideration to change the team style to accommodate these players more effectively.

# Enter a Swedish pragmatist

From 2002 – 2006 the talent of the England national team was evident. Yet whenever they faced a team on a similar level; whether Brazil or Portugal, the team's failings were exposed by their tactical naivety. To the frustration of many – the England manager Sven-Goran Eriksson consistently went for the basic 4-4-2 which meant that the chosen dynamic central midfield pairing (most often Steven Gerrard and Frank Lampard) was continually undermined by a lack of tactical awareness, which in turn often exposed the central defensive partnership.

At their clubs both Gerrard and Lampard were the attacking midfielders who would score and create goals for others. Their managers, notably Rafa Benitez and Jose Mourinho, had made sure the team accommodated the attacking talents of their English stars. Both Lampard and Gerrard were therefore supported by a defensive midfielder or two who would provide cover and support to their attacking midfielder.

In players such as Claude Makelele and Michael Essien at Chelsea and Dieter Hamann and Xavi Alonso for Liverpool, Lampard and Gerrard were given freedom to attack. For England this support and cover simply did not exist. Both players wanted to support the attack like they did for their clubs and looked unwilling or incapable of being more disciplined and provide defensive support for the team. It meant that both players' performances suffered when playing for England and that England's midfield was overrun and overloaded in many games.

It appeared obvious that in order to bring out the best in players like Gerrard and Lampard, as well as providing the team with more stability and balance, England needed a tactical revolution. It was obvious that England possessed a group of players crying out for a 4-2-3-1 system. It would have allowed more freedom, more expression and allowed England to overload the midfield and to potentially dominate games.

Yet this was not the thinking of the English FA or their manager. After decades of failure they had chosen a manager in Eriksson who was more 'English' than either Venables or Hoddle.

When looking at Eriksson's development as a coach there is no surprise why the English FA chose him to lead the England national team; Eriksson chose to use the 4-4-2 because he was actually a very strong 'Anglophile'. As a young coach in Sweden, Eriksson had witnessed the success of a 'new style' of football which had proven hugely successful.

Two English coaches called Bobby Houghton and Roy Hodgson, both whom had developed their coaching under the tutelage of Allen Wade, were appointed managers of Malmo and Halmstads in Sweden's top league during the 1970's. It was the classic English style of 4-4-2, high pressing and direct passes. It was not 'pretty' but it was very effective. To highlight the impressive work of both coaches between 1974 and 1979 Malmo and Halmstads would win five out of six league titles. And incredibly Houghton would take Malmo to the European Cup final in 1979, losing to Brian Clough's Nottingham Forest.

Eriksson had observed Houghton and Hodgson's style and success and became a believer in their methods. As Jonathan Wilson pointed out, "The success they had achieved convinced the young Swede that this was a style worth developing." Eriksson would take over at IFK Göteborg and would instil the principles of Houghton and Hodgson with his team. More tactical awareness, high work rate, and less creativity was his approach. Through this style Eriksson would take Göteborg to league, cup and UEFA cup success in 1982, seemingly confounding his critics.

This success would later take Eriksson around Europe coaching sides like Benfica, Roma, Sampdoria and Lazio. When he was offered the England national job it was almost a spiritual union for the Swede.

> Many anticipated that Eriksson would bring a European style to the side; in fact they got a man whose career had been built on the rigid 4-4-2 learnt from the disciples of Allen Wade!

Eriksson had a genuine chance with the Golden Generation yet would not deviate from the traditional system of English football. Under Eriksson, England continued to play the 4-4-2 against sides like Brazil in 2002. It was not even a 4-4-1-1. He relied on the 'big man, little striker' combination in Emile Heskey and Michael Owen which denied England the chance to use any of their creative playmakers such as Paul Scholes, Joe Cole or Steven Gerrard.

In a time when the number ten was becoming more important to the modern game, through players like Alessandro Del Piero, Zinedine Zidane, and Dennis Bergkamp, England refused to adapt and evolve. Their stubborn approach was once again their failing as it had been for the past several decades. A change in style would have allowed England the opportunity to find places for some of their most talented players. England's pigeon holing problem remained.

Perhaps the arrival of Wayne Rooney would give England that added dimension which had been lacking for so long. He was regarded as the brightest talent to come out of England for many years and he announced his talent with a world class goal for Everton against Arsenal in October 2002, five days before he turned 17. Rooney was clearly a special player and his talent prompted Arsenal's manager Arsene Wenger to proclaim to the BBC that Rooney, "is the biggest England talent I've seen since I arrived in England. There has certainly not been a player under 20 as good as him since I became a manager here."

At the European Championships in 2004 Rooney's emergence would appear to point at a new era for English football. Rooney would score four goals in the tournament and would offer England what they had been lacking. He dropped into deeper positions to collect the ball and would drive at the opposition with confidence and control. However Rooney would be injured in the game against Portugal and England's hopes would be dashed again.

> With Rooney, England appeared to have found a player who could offer them an approach befitting the modern game.

Two years later, and after moving to Manchester United, Rooney was now deployed very much as a number nine. In the repeat of the game against Portugal, at the 2006 World Cup, he was used as a sole striker in a 4-5-1 formation where he found himself isolated and frustrated, and his sending off for stamping was no surprise. The truth was that his talents were not being used effectively by Eriksson and England suffered accordingly.

Rooney is evidently a player who could have been what Zidane, Del Piero and Bergkamp were for their countries. The playmaker who controls and conducts the game. However, he was left isolated too often by being asked to play the 'classic' number nine role, when he offered so much more to the England side. And it has not just been Rooney who has suffered from being played out of position, the regular failings of England in the major tournaments have come because of a continuous inability to accommodate and utilise talent appropriately.

## A failure to accommodate the best talent

Brian Clough, who according to many was the 'best England manager never had', wrote about how, if he had been the manager, he would have revolved the side around Glenn Hoddle:

In his autobiography Clough lamented the neglect of Hoddle from the English national team, "How could successive England managers have failed to see what Hoddle could have done for the team? His beautiful touch and control, limitless vision for the exquisite ball nobody else anticipated, his wonderful gift for the telling pass – what more can any manager require? What chance do you have if you cannot recognise a footballer who is capable of winning matches?"

Glenn Hoddle, however, was a player who went against the beliefs of the English FA's direct football doctrine. He was a player with skill, creativity and vision. As a player and coach he went against the views of Wade and Hughes and their safety first approach. Their lack of understanding about the game led to a philosophy which distrusted ability and skill, favouring instead a thoughtless physicality and work rate.

These characteristics would define England's style and approach and would be the blueprint for future generations. A neglect, or more importantly a restriction, on players like Hoddle as well as Peter Beardsley, Kevin Keegan, Chris Waddle and not to mention Paul Gascoigne whose 57 caps spanning a decade appear a waste of such talent point to an issue with successive England managers. The team and the style should have been moulded and centred *around* these 'types' of players.

And this brings us to Paul Scholes. Without question the Hoddle of his generation. When Paul Scholes played in the Champions League final in 2011 - both Xavi and Iniesta were desperate for his shirt. For them Paul Scholes was their inspiration. The best two midfielders of their generation had grown up watching Paul Scholes. In fact they were instructed at La Masia, Barcelona's youth academy, to learn from this English maestro.

Yet Scholes would retire from English national football in 2004 after just 66 caps. One of the greatest midfielders that England has produced, like Hoddle, he had been very much undervalued for England, especially under Eriksson.

In an interview with the *Daily Mail,* Xavi commented that, "In the last 15 to 20 years the best central midfielder that I have seen - the most complete - is Scholes." He went on to make the assertion that, "If he had been Spanish then maybe he would have been valued more."

Why did a player like Scholes, with so much class, have to retire so young? His reasons were simple; he was not used effectively. Before, we spoke about how Eriksson had failed to get the best out of Wayne Rooney and the same was true of Scholes. In his autobiography, Steven Gerrard talks about how Scholes was moved out to the left in Euro 2004 in order to accommodate Lampard in the central attacking role. As Gerrard wrote, when Eriksson announced Scholes would be playing out left against France, "I felt sorry for Scholesy, who got the graveyard shift." The graveyard shift? For one of England's finest playmakers?

It appears that changing the formation to accommodate the players and their talents was not a possibility for Eriksson. Instead England would suffer because their best players would be played out of position… playing in a formation which had been proven to be a failure.

Playing Scholes on the left side of midfield had reduced his influence on the game and, in trying to 'fit' players into a functional 4-4-2, Eriksson had lost the best England player of that generation.

Xavi is a great example of a player who shows what 'could' have been achieved had Scholes been used as the focal point of the team. Spain has found a system which suits the skills of Xavi and which has seen them dominate world football.

> Lessons must be learnt from Paul Scholes' England career - about how to get the best out of quality players.

Now when people talk of the 'Golden Generation' Michael Carrick is never mentioned. It is not surprising considering he has only played 29 times for England. Amazingly his debut for England came in 2001 and yet he has never been a regular fixture in England's squad for over a decade.

This is somewhat remarkable considering that, since 2006, he has been playing for one of the world's best sides - winning domestic and European trophies. Carrick's vision, passing and movement became invaluable for his club and his arrival would spark years of success for Manchester United.

Is it *not* amazing that one of the world's best managers has used Carrick as his main midfielder in what has been one of United's most successful periods? Yet Carrick has not been deemed good enough for England?

When you actually see United play, you see how effective Carrick is and how important he is to the balance and tempo of the team. His intelligence, vision and movement mean he supplies the attack and supports the team defensively. You don't see Carrick tearing all over the pitch; you don't see him getting irate at players and officials. He is a true professional and one who must be a great player to have in any side.

Imagine what could have been - had Carrick been the hub of England's midfield, supplying the attack and staying disciplined in his position, providing balance for the whole side. You can only imagine what might have happened if England's midfield had been a 4-2-3-1 with Carrick and Scholes controlling the game.

English football's failings are that players like Scholes, Carrick and Hoddle were neglected because they did not portray the 'English values' which were developed by Charles Hughes. International football, like European football, is *different* to the Premier League. The Premier League values high tempo and direct play. Yet in European and international football the game is more controlled and balanced. Discipline is the key to being successful. And these players would have been ideal for England to exercise discipline and control over matches.

If Carrick was Italian, Spanish, or German, he would be in their sides; he resembles Andrea Pirlo, Xabi Alonso and Bastian Schweinsteiger - players who English fans lavish so much praise on. Yet the naive and ignorant do not see that, for the past several decades, England has possessed these types of players – they were simply restricted based on a nation's culture and philosophy on how football should be played.

# A nation going backwards

The England manager's role is very much a poisoned chalice where the occupant of the role becomes scrutinised to the nth degree, and ultimately vilified for his performance. It is almost impossible to succeed in the position as the expectations are 'unrealistic'.

Yet for the past twenty years each change of coach has not improved results and performances. England has continued to underperform and 'fail' on the big stage. Questions surrounding poor performances and results have been asked predominantly of the manager and players however it has been the failings of the FA's methods which can be seen to be the issue across the past decades.

As we saw Wade and Hughes did not value possession because it did not create goal scoring opportunities yet they failed to understand that it is almost essential for success. This failed philosophy is perhaps the biggest reason for England's failure.

England's national team has constantly failed in major tournaments because of players' individual technical deficiencies and the team's inability to retain possession for any substantial amount of time. As well as this, playing a high octane style of constant pressing and quick tempo football has proved counter-productive to achieving success on the international stage.

The style of play has relied on 'percentages' rather than genuine skill, craft and quality and whilst it cannot be characterised as 'wasteful' - it is not conducive to international tournaments. The need and mindset to attack at all times has not only been punished by teams who could keep the ball - it has proved severely fatiguing. This is especially true during the summer months when international tournaments take place in hotter climates, which have rendered England's 'energetic' style even more futile.

Yet time and time again the problem is that England has not attempted to learn and adapt from this glaring truth.

> Against the lesser national sides, especially in qualifying
> groups England did well yet when they
> came up against a side who were regarded
> as an equal, they most often lost.

These failings were seen under Fabio Capello also; a 1-0 loss to France in 2008 and a 2-0 defeat by Spain in 2009 highlighted the significant gap between England and Europe's top nations. The team would be shown up again in the latter part of 2009 when both Ukraine and Brazil defeated England 1-0. It signified England's approach to international football; a safety first, defensive mentality.

The final straw for England's failings came at the 2010 World Cup. Much was expected, once again, of England yet this time they were not only shamed by their old rivals Germany, but were also completely outplayed by Algeria. Yes, Algeria.

The Algerians looked more composed in possession, played with more confidence and were the side most disappointed to get only a draw in the group game. That match made clear that England's Golden Generation was at its end. The pressing concern was what lay next.

The 4-1 loss to Germany was the nail in the coffin; Germany's high tempo, counter attacking game was too much for the old legs of England. England were made to look like amateurs and whereas the losses to Portugal in 2004 and 2006, and perhaps even Brazil in 2002, could be deemed 'close' games, this one showed the huge gulf in class between England and the best.

> In under a decade English football had actually gone
> backwards, or more precisely, other nations had moved
> forward and left England behind.

## Summary

The basis of these opening chapters has been to indicate how the problems of poor decision making and a misguided vision have negatively influenced English national football.

This first part has highlighted the issues which have affected the senior side and the reasons for England's failure. At the end, the national team is only ever the beneficiary of whatever work has been done elsewhere. If something starts badly, it will not end well.

## Chapter 4

The foundations on which England has developed players and teams these past several decades were fundamentally wrong. These foundations have developed poor coaches and players and for decades the English style has been outdated. These constant failings have not been properly addressed.

The truth is that Charles Hughes' philosophy laid down foundations which would be to the detriment of English football. The failure to develop coaches who would teach their players to be comfortable on the ball and to keep possession, instead of direct football and physicality has been the English FA's 'legacy'.

The problems are seen not just with the senior game but also at the grassroots. The 'copycat' approach to youth football has seen the same inflexible formations and mentalities continued; young player development has often been tarnished and damaged by poor coaches and old school methods.

A focus on physicality and hard work over skill and creativity has reduced the quality of English players leading to an influx of more talented foreign players. English clubs see more talent abroad than at home, a problem which has been exacerbated over the past decade due to the FA's poor planning and lack of innovation.

English football is now in a crisis which has been neglected for too long. The following chapters will dig deeper into why this is the case.

# Part II

# Developing The Player

# 5

# A Crisis in the Development of English Quality

*"What I believe we must all accept is that for a country of some 60 million people we are not producing the depth of players at the top level with the necessary technical skills required by the major clubs and international teams."*
Trevor Brooking.

## A lack of genuine talent

From the Hughes philosophy, English football valued hard work and determination over technical skill and intelligence. The last ditch and crunching tackles, where the ball flies out of play, became something to value and cheer. More praise was seemingly given to those players who booted the ball into the stands than those who looked to pass to their teammates.

Is it a real surprise, therefore, that English football has not produced a large quantity of world class players and coaches? During the Allen Wade and Charles Hughes era, English football would develop not only direct-style coaches but it would be required to develop players suited to this style.

Through a philosophy which developed direct football, a certain type of player was necessary. The big centre forward became essential; he would head the ball on, bring the ball down and create chances for his side. At the other end would be a big strong central defender who could battle and challenge for these long high balls and who could also lump the ball 60 yards to his giant forward.

Direct football required direct players, it meant that the midfield area was rarely contested and there was no place in the 'trenches' for skill or genuine creativity. Any of those small, technical players were deemed surplus to requirements as, according to Hughes' philosophy, the game was built for physical 'giants'.

# Lilleshall - The FA School of excellence

Charles Hughes not only wrote books and developed philosophies; he also developed and formed the FA's school of excellence in order to improve the qualities of the best young schoolboys in England.

From 1984 to 1999 the FA would select the best 16 schoolboys at 14 years old and educate them at the school of excellence at Lilleshall for two years.

In many ways it was a positive step for England's youth development. A 'school' of football where players would receive more coaching sounded good in principle. And it may have been a great idea which could have developed a new generation of players as well as coaches for the modern game.

But as we know, the philosophy of Hughes and the FA was not about skill, creativity or individuality. They wanted workhouse athletes, players who could run all day and tackle hard. Thus the selection process centred around those requirements. Any ideas of skill, creativity and technical quality were not only ignored but actually treated with caution. As Jonathan Wilson wrote, about Hughes and philosophy, "Skill or anything that required thinking too much, was not to be trusted, while 'physical toughness' remained the ultimate virtue."

John Cartwright was a former professional footballer and coach who was brought in to Lilleshall, as technical director in the late 1980s, to develop players' ability with the ball. Yet he states he was never involved in the selection process, as the emphasis was on big strong athletes.

As he pointed out in an interview with *FourFourTwo*, "The prevailing philosophy in English football at the time was about getting the ball forward as quickly as possible." He saw how a premium was put on bigger players at 14 years old who possessed strength and athleticism. This saw players like Jamie Carragher, Sol Campbell and Wes Brown come through the school and interestingly saw a player like Steven Gerrard rejected because he was 'too small'.

Towards the end of the school's existence Cartwright did start to see a shift towards smaller players. Players like Michael Owen, Andy Cole, Nick Barmby and Jermaine Defoe were recruited. Yet as you can see from these players, and their careers in football, they were the perfect foil for the direct style; fast forwards who could feed off the flick-ons from their giant centre forward. They were finishers to 'direct football'. It was not revolution but evolution.

The failings of the school of excellence are clear. Recruitment was based on a flawed vision and philosophy. Size, strength and speed are all important components for football yet surely skill, vision and intelligence are more essential?

In recent years Cartwright has been a major critic of English football's historical approach. For Cartwright, the issues of England's youth development come from the "outdated coaching methods" which we have discussed already. In his book, *Football for the Brave*, he talks about England's reliance on physicality, on the 'athletic bruiser' who is preferred over the skilful players; physical presence supersedes skill because 'winning is everything'.

## Summary

As part one highlighted, England's failings go much deeper than the 'Golden Generation', they go to the root of youth development. Compared to other countries England is far behind in producing talent capable of playing in the modern game with the culture of English football heavily affected by the philosophies of the FA and their coaching methods.

A thrashing by Germany in the 2010 World Cup awoke many to the problems plaguing England's issues in international football. It is apparent that England cannot compete with Spain, Germany or Holland. So how can we improve our national side? The key must be youth development.

After that defeat to Germany, after a decade of disappointment and failed hopes, real questions were finally being asked of youth development in this country.

England's problem is that we have sought to develop 'top down' far too often. The money goes from the top and trickles down, leaving barely anything to really improve the standards at the bottom, the 'grassroots'. Grassroots is the first step for developing players suited for the modern game. This is where the foundations are set and where players for the future are developed.

# 6

# The Charter for Quality

*"I'm looking for England to produce players capable of winning the World Cup and playing for their club teams and dominating Europe in the European club competitions."*
Howard Wilkinson. *Charter for Quality*, 1997.

## A solution to England's problems

During the 1990's a frenzy of 'soul searching' in the national game had been created. After the poor performance at the 1992 European Championships and failure to qualify for the 1994 World Cup, concerns were raised about the relative lack of technical ability in the English game compared to other European nations.

In 1997, concerned that English football was falling behind in terms of youth development, the FA brought in Howard Wilkinson who, after an extensive evaluation of English football's youth development plan, launched the Football Association's crusade to improve the quality of English born footballers.

Wilkinson issued an ambitious and largely admirable set of proposals which would seek to change the way that English players were developed.

As Technical Director at the FA, Wilkinson was commissioned to undertake a comprehensive review of the existing youth development *structure* at the time. This review laid the foundations for the *Charter for Quality*. Wilkinson was adamant that dealing with these problems was a key priority for English football and his position as Technical Director.

In the Charter he admitted that, "A number of countries woke up to what was possible before us - Holland, followed by France, but also Norway and some of the old iron curtain countries. They realised that the old tried and trusted methods were not the best." Accordingly, Wilkinson came up with a model which was heavily influenced by other nations, notably as Stephen Wagg points out, Gerard Houllier's work at the French national academy at Clairefontaine.

Wilkinson had spoken highly of Manchester United who, during the 1990's, had produced a core of young players to make any academy around the world jealous; David Beckham, Paul Scholes and Gary Neville were just some of those who came through at that time. In turn Liverpool, according to Wilkinson, were providing 'good practice' and he wanted to see this replicated across the country.

Wilkinson intended to establish more of these 'academies' at all Premier League clubs. Now whether the FA school of excellence at Lilleshall was indeed providing 'good practice', or not, is open for debate when considering how it was recruiting players and developing them under the methodology of Charles Hughes and the English FA. However, it was evident that they *were* developing players for the professional game. For Wilkinson, the establishment of more academies by the leading professional clubs would lead (theoretically) to an improvement in the talent pool. Thus Premier League clubs were instructed that opening an academy would become mandatory.

In his report, Wilkinson put forward some serious concerns and issues with the then current youth development system. His belief was that a focus on 'winning games' only encouraged clubs to recruit the biggest and strongest boys and they neglected the smaller players. Wilkinson's *Charter for Quality* described a national academy system from grassroots level which would pay greater attention to developing individuals' 'technical education'.

The most important aspect to the new system for Wilkinson was that more young players would be trained by more 'specialist' coaches. As Stephen Wagg says, "Wilkinson felt that too many children were reliant on well-meaning parents and unqualified coaches for their football development," and Wilkinson believed this was hampering their progress as well as affecting their 'well-being'. Therefore he sought to change the age that academies could bring in players, allowing clubs to recruit players from nine years old compared to the previous 14.

Wilkinson's aim was to provide more young players with high level coaching and facilities as well as catering for their well-being, and educational and social welfare - a 'holistic' approach to a child's development.

Wilkinson also saw the need to have smaller pitches and small sided teams of 5v5 or 7v7 in order to improve the technical development of players. Developing skills was a major part of his vision. Wilkinson's intentions were clear and honest; to develop talented footballers and, importantly, more of them. For him if the Charter was implemented properly, England would develop far greater numbers of quality players than previously.

However the actual implementation of the Charter was seen as somewhat 'watered down' and there were serious problems which prevented the Charter from being implemented fully across England.

> Wilkinson's vision was to emulate what France had done and revolutionise the youth development system – yet his vision was ultimately 'watered down'.

## Problems which arose

Upon reflection, Wilkinson admitted that the implementation of the Charter did not turn out quite as he had planned. He admitted that, "I only envisaged 12 to 14 academies, but we finished up with 40, which in my humble opinion was always too many. I didn't think the country had enough talent to support 40 high-level development centres."

Although Wilkinson proposed some important improvements to the academy system, the problem was that too many clubs ignored or neglected much of the Charter. The lack of regimented rules put on academies meant that the standards proposed by Wilkinson were not monitored or maintained. More observation and management of the academies could have meant improved standards and a higher production of quality domestic players.

> Wilkinson's Charter was seen more like guidelines rather than a strict policy of youth development.

Wilkinson's Charter could have been revolutionary for English football yet Wilkinson, speaking to the BBC, believed that the powerful influence of the Premier League, coupled with in-fighting, at the FA diluted his blueprint's effectiveness.

It would take until the disappointing failure to qualify for the 2008 European Championships to see a new vision put forward that would seek to improve standards. That defeat to Croatia at Wembley in 2007 would be the spark which ignited the necessity for change.

# The new and improved version

*"We must raise standards, not implement something that would create a broader pool of average players rather than a deeper one of the right level of talent."*
Premier League statement in 2008.

In what could be seen as a landmark day for youth development in England, on Thursday the 23rd of October 2011, the 72 Football League clubs voted in favour of the 'Elite Player Performance Plan' (EPPP), a 'radical new overhaul' of the current national youth system.

The EPPP was a plan drawn up by both the FA and the Premier League with the aim of developing more top level players for the English Premier League and the England national team. The Premier League's Youth Director, Ged Roddy, who reviewed the academy system and developed the EPPP, set out with the intention to put English youngsters 'on a par with continental contemporaries'. The view of the creators of the plan was that foreign clubs are coaching their players to a higher standard than England's 'outdated' system allows.

The philosophy behind the EPPP is straightforward, "[to] create a system that puts the player at the heart of the development process and give them the best opportunities in terms of coaching, access and education."

The Premier League published the principles upon which the EPPP was designed, and they were as follows:

- Increase the number and quality of Home Grown Players gaining professional contracts in clubs and playing first-team football at the highest level
- Create more time for players to play and be coached
- Improve coaching provision
- Implement a system of effective measurement and Quality Assurance
- Positively influence strategic investment into the Academy System, demonstrating value for money
- Seek to implement significant gains in every aspect of player development

The aims and intentions, which appear positive and promising, look very similar to the aims of Wilkinson in 1997. Many were asking if the same issues would occur once again.

# Significant changes

After being appointed as Director of Youth at the Premier League in 2010 Roddy carried out an immediate audit of what was happening within the academy structure across the game. One of the biggest things that struck him was the lack of contact time between players and coaches. His proposal was that the more contact time there is, the better.

Although the previous decade had successfully facilitated increased contact time, the amount of coaching time English youngsters received still paled into insignificance when compared to the coaching time received by continental counterparts.

According to an article in *The Daily Telegraph*, there is a significant difference between Europe's top nations in terms of the amount of contact time young footballers receive in academies between the ages of 9 and 21.

| COUNTRY | CONTACT TIME (HOURS) |
|---------|----------------------|
| SPAIN | 4,880 |
| HOLLAND | 5,740 |
| FRANCE | 5,940 |
| ENGLAND | 3,760 |

The new plan aimed to improve youth development by allowing clubs to have more coaching time with their young players.

# Category/Tier formation

As well as increased coaching hours, a revolutionary new 'category' or 'tier' formulation was introduced where clubs' youth systems were ranked according to how many staff an academy employs and how much money they spend on their youth development.

It was proposed that there would be four grades of academy, with the highest rated academies being able to sign the best players and command the largest fees. The top graded academies, Category One, would have high contact time with young players, employ a minimum of 18 full-time staff, and manage an operational budget of £2.5m. These coaches would coach for four times as long as other academies and players would benefit from the world class facilities that only the best clubs can afford.

As well as this the academy needed to have a coaching programme and philosophy in place which goes throughout the club. To be Category One an academy needs to have a full-time programme for Under-15's and 16's which, in 2014/15, will be extended down to Under-12's.

For Roddy it was important that the mistakes of Wilkinson's *Charter for Quality* were not made again. The key this time around is to include independent audits and follow up visits to make sure that quality and standards are maintained.

Roddy and his colleagues want to ensure that if an academy gets Category One status, it operates as one.

# 90 minute rule

The new rules have also abolished the previous '90-minute' rule where academies were only allowed to sign Under 18 players if they reside within 90 minutes travel of the training facility. This had historically provided each club with a 'catchment area', and it was set up to prevent larger clubs from taking youth players away from home at a young age for training.

However, the new rules see the advantage of top players playing together, instead of being dispersed across dozens of centres. They will allow clubs that have earned a Category One grade to recruit young talent from further afield than is permitted under the current rules. Effectively a Category One ranking gives clubs the licence to recruit the top youth players right across the country. The writers of the plan feel that there are too many talented players dispersed across different academies and believe that if those talented players were to all be at Category One academies, then their development will excel.

At the other end of the scale will be the Category Four academies, acting as a 'safety net' and only allowed to pick up previously failed youth players at the age of 16. Category Three academies will have no contact with youth players until the age of 11. Category Two academies offer less coaching hours than the top academies yet will have the same freedom to recruit players from four years old and sign them at nine.

# A concern from the lower leagues

As seen, under the new rules, academies who qualify for Category One status will be able to select youngsters from a pool of nationwide talent and those already contracted to another club will be able to leave for minimal compensation.

A Category One academy will have the freedom to select any player playing from a Category Two, Three or Four academy; all that will be required is for the club to contact the other club and inform them that they are coming to see the player. This will prevent clubs from holding on to their players, a strategy which has previously generated a lot of criticism.

Critics of the EPPP have suggested that the rules are very much skewed in favour of the Premier League, at the expense of Football League clubs. The new deal will see every club receive an increase in their funding for a guaranteed four-year period, with the amount determined by their academy status. The Premier League provides £5million in funding for Football League clubs to put into youth football, and this played a big part in the EPPP being voted through. 46 of the 72 clubs voted for it because that money is crucial for them. Effectively the Premier League could have withdrawn this funding if they did not agree to the changes. It is hard not to view the deal as underpinned by 'bullying' and blackmail.

Critics of the plan point towards the new compensation ruling - which only benefits the richest clubs. Simon Jordan, the former Crystal Palace chairman wrote in *The Guardian* in 2011, after the EPPP was agreed, "The Football League has been blackmailed by the Premier League into accepting these radical new proposals which will allow the richest clubs to 'cherry-pick' the best young talent for a fraction of their worth."

What these new rules mean is that Premier League clubs will no longer have to pay substantial fees for the best young talent in the Football League. Instead of the previous tribunal system, there will now be a fixed tariff in place to determine the fee a club must pay for a youth player. It is £3,000 per year for a player aged between 9 and 11, with the fee from 12 to 16-year-olds ranging between £12,500 and £40,000, dependent on a club's youth category.

This is a long way off the £5 million that Leeds received for Tom Taiwo and Michael Woods from Chelsea (both of whose careers suffered after moving to Chelsea).

Liverpool reportedly shelled out an initial £1.5m to MK Dons for 14-year-old Oluwaseyi Ojo in November 2011. Under the new system they would be able to buy him for less than £150,000. Crystal Palace received £700,000 for John Bostock, however with the new rules they would receive no more than £100,000.

This is a significant change and clearly will have major implications for many of the lower league academies or centres of excellence. Many of the Football League Academies have become reliant on the sale of their young starlets, or indeed the compensation awarded, in order to generate money, keep the youth academy going, and to stay afloat. The concern from many is that the new rules will force some clubs to close down their academies completely.

For the lower league academies these plans may just make them reconsider the value and need of having a youth academy. There may be a growing tendency for clubs to ditch their academies altogether and pad out their squads with players rejected by the elite at an older age. Burnley has already closed its centre of excellence due to the new rules, claiming that it is just not viable to keep it going. It is estimated that between 30 and 40 youth academies, of different levels, may follow suit.

If these lower League academies do shut down, then we could be in serious jeopardy of losing potential England internationals; England regulars Tom Cleverley and Joe Hart came from Bradford City and Shrewsbury Town respectively before going to the top Manchester sides.

The Premier League is adamant that the EPPP is a 'fair system' and the reforms are necessary. But they could cause a long-term problem that will transform the landscape of youth development in the Football League. These are massive changes in the game.

# What will the future bring?

The cynics have a strong case against the EPPP yet it is hard not to argue with the new plans. The EPPP is not a guarantee of success but there is logic behind the changes and it is hard not to disagree with the fundamental need to improve the standards of academies in England.

If anything, these new plans have forced academies to assess what they are doing in terms of developing players: the level of coaching, having a coaching philosophy, and creating a positive environment for the players. From the many stories heard across the country, the EPPP has highlighted that England's elite youth development was, on the whole, more amateur than professional. A change was very much needed.

Howard Wilkinson was critical of the number of academies which were created after his Charter, believing that he didn't think the country had enough talent to support 40 *high-level* development centres. By seeking to have a tier system, the new proposals are aiming to follow through with Wilkinson's original aims and have closer to twenty high quality academies which will work with a higher proportion of the top talent in England. Elite levels of professional development will be required if we wish to produce more elite level players.

In a similar fashion to the philosophy behind Lilleshall, the best players in the country will be playing together, learning together and developing under high levels of coaching and world class facilities.

> For the past decade too much talent has been dispersed across too many academies. The new proposals, therefore, make sense in bringing more of that talent together.

We will not see the real fruits of the EPPP for years, perhaps even decades and it may be that the new intake of nine-year-olds will be the first true post EPPP group.

This will mean it will be a decade until these players are seen in the professional game. Patience is necessary and essential.

However, there are issues which the EPPP has failed to address. The plans have centred around what the academies are doing in terms of coaching, philosophy and facilities, yet they appear to ignore or neglect what is happening beneath the academy level.

If England truly wants to improve its youth development and produce more players, then there are deeper issues, such as what is happening at the grassroots level in terms of the environment, and the level of coaching the players are receiving.

In the next chapter we shall start by looking at the 'golden years' of player development (not to be confused with the Golden Generation!) – a key time which needs to be addressed *before a player even reaches an academy.*

# 7

# The Magic Number of Greatness

In England we marvel at the talent of players like Lionel Messi and Cristiano Ronaldo and many other foreign players who appear to possess such natural football skill and talent. We wonder how they became so great and, importantly, we ask why England does not produce more of these players.

Based on this question there have come dozens of books on ways to develop talent – some of which offer new methods, ideas and beliefs about developing elite individuals. Largely, the conclusion is that these individuals are not 'natural talents' but, in fact, the products of a number of factors which have contributed to their rise to an elite level.

## The 10,000 hour rule

Firstly, we must begin with a Swedish psychologist called Anders Ericsson. Ericsson is widely recognized as one of the world's leading experts on expertise and his research has seen him cover a wide array of domains including medicine, music, chess, and sports. Through his research he has found that the classic view on skill learning, which is "based on the assumption that innate biological capacities limit the level of achievement that a person can attain," is a falsehood.

In fact, Ericsson and his colleagues have discovered that becoming an expert in anything is not 'natural', but down to how much practice a person carries out. This principle, according to Ericsson, applies to all domains including sports, chess and music. From his research Ericsson has found that all performers, including the most 'gifted' or 'talented' need a "minimum of approximately ten years of intense involvement before they reach an international level."

> Ericsson found that professional development is completed only after years or even decades of experience.

Ericsson's research led to what has become known as the 'ten year rule' which, although it can be seen as a reliable indicator of expertise, is not actually set in stone. In Ericsson's opinion most elite performers, in fact, take considerably longer to reach an elite level.

Ericsson actually found that it was not 'years' but 'hours' which mattered the most. In one of his earliest, and most famous, pieces of research he conducted a study on violinists – examining the amount of practice they had accrued over their careers, and how many hours they had put in since they started playing the violin. His results found a significant trend, one which would revolutionize previous ideas of expertise.

What Ericsson found was amazing; those who had practiced 8,000 hours were deemed 'good' performers and those who had practiced for roughly 4,000 hours became music teachers. The violinists who had accrued 10,000 hours of practice were the ones who reached world class levels. When Ericsson studied other skills and disciplines he found the same formula. The top professionals increased their practice time year after year and after about ten years they had reached 10,000 hours.

> Significantly, researchers have never found a 'natural' – it is practice which is the key.

# A lack of practice

In the previous chapter we saw that the new plans by the Premier League, put in place by Ged Roddy, sought to increase the amount of contact time football players in English academies enjoyed. Roddy was well aware of Ericsson's magic number. Yet if we base the development of world class talent on the 10,000 hour rule then concerns emerge. The amount of professional coaching which English youngsters in academy football receive does not allow them to get anywhere near 10,000 hours!

We saw, in the previous chapter, that English players receive only 3,760 hours of practice in academies between the ages of 9 and 21. The difficulty in football, especially in England, is that many players struggle to get even close to 4,000 by the time they are 16. If we take the 10,000 hour rule as our guide to producing top class footballers, then we have to seriously look at how we can get more players playing more often.

On the flip side, the same lack of hours is true of young footballers in Spain (4,880 hours) Holland (5,740 hours) and France (5,940 hours). On these figures, no country is reaching the hours necessary for achieving greatness yet they continue to produce more and more talented players than England.

It is clear that a player's practice time and development must involve hours accrued 'outside' what academies offer. So while the EPPP, in its quest to increase contact time, has sought to increase practice hours in academies, there is clearly more that needs to happen in order for players to increase their practice time outside of the academy environment.

The EPPP report has neglected key factors which have the potential to push our players up to the key number. Its focus has been on what academies can offer players, yet has not taken into account other areas which are almost essential for young players to develop. As the following sections will highlight, academies will not be able to do it alone...

# The Golden Years

In England's quest to increase the practice time of young players, could the answer be in the period which former Arsenal and Holland international Dennis Bergkamp calls the "the golden period of learning"?

Based on the research from Ericsson it is clear that the key to developing world class performers is to start young. It was found that an individual's introduction to training, in traditional domains of expertise, occurs at around five to ten years of age. Interestingly, research by Lenroot and Geidd (2006) has found that between the ages of 5 and 11 a child develops 95% of their neural development. 95%!

> Skills that are learned between 5 and 11 will
> (near enough) dictate a child's future.

It is no surprise to learn that world class performers such as Tiger Woods and Lionel Messi were developing their particular skills from a very young age.
It doesn't just seem important to start early, it seems necessary.

In his book, *The Talent Code*, Dan Coyle highlights the importance of these golden years believing that the first decade of life is paramount to fulfilling any potential that a child has. Coyle points out that the more a young child repeats and practices a particular skill, the faster the brain sends signals through our neurons and synaptic connections. This builds up insulation, called myelin, around these skill circuits and, for many researchers, understanding how and why myelin develops could allow researchers and coaches to develop more world class performers.

According to Coyle there is, "…nothing more effective in building skill than executing the action, firing the impulse down the nerve fibres, and honing the circuit." Ultimately the key is practice; the more you practice, the more you fire those specific signals, and the more myelin that builds up.

Effectively the more a young player repeats movements and actions the more it helps the brain and muscles remember what to do. More automatic movements are produced which require less conscious thought. Those young children who are constantly practicing begin to master the skill and become more efficient at it.

> Through practice and repetition a young child begins to develop more automaticity, which leads to a greater quickness and fluency in their movement.

What Coyle argues, along with the findings of Ericsson, is that action is key. The skill will not develop without practice, and more practice.

So, if these golden years are so important for a young footballer's development, what are we, as a nation, doing about them?

## Deliberate practice

It is not just 'practice' which will help develop elite players. Anders Ericsson believes that the most dramatic improvements in the level of performance found in sports are associated with an improved quality and quantity of practice; he defines this as 'deliberate practice'.

For Ericsson the key to developing elite levels of performance is, "Primarily attributable to the environmental conditions necessary for its slow emergence, and to the years of deliberate practice required to develop the complex mediating mechanisms that support expertise." He believes that players need to be pushed and stretched to achieve excellence and that deliberate practice requires much effort, focus, and involves making mistakes.

This idea of deliberate practice makes a lot of sense when we consider the need to challenge skills in order to make progress. It points towards an issue which has caused much debate in recent years in England when considering why there is a dearth of talented footballers: the death of 'street soccer'.

In the past, young children would develop their physical, technical and social skills outside, playing with their friends in their community, or in parks, or at school. Endless hours would be spent being 'active'. These hours of 'fun', in fact, prove vital in building up and developing a child's potential, wrapping myelin around those skills they were practicing. The environment would be just what Ericsson would wish for elite development; focused, replete with hard work, and challenging. Is this the case now? Unfortunately not.

Young children now are 'blessed' with technology and entertained for hour upon hour by computers and television. A recent study by Dr. Gavin Sandercock, a children's fitness expert at Essex University, found that children are becoming "weaker, less muscular and unable to do physical tasks that previous generations found simple." He found that a generation dedicated to online pursuits has led to 10-year-olds with "declining strength and an inability to grip an object firmly."

Sandercock argues that changes in activity patterns among English youngsters, such as a reduction in rope-climbing in P.E., and tree-climbing for fun, have prevented children from developing strength. In effect, children are becoming more unfit, less active, more sedentary and, in many cases, heavier than before.

> Children are not as active as they used to be,
> and this is affecting their development.

From a football perspective – this is a major concern. Less activity means less skill being developed - resulting in young children wasting the key years of development. Academy football does not start (officially) until the age of 9, yet it has been proven that between the ages of 5 and 11 a young player needs to build a solid foundation. This is not happening well enough.

It is clear that the golden years in a child's development are essential - so are we giving our children and our potential footballers the best chances and opportunities? How astonishing that we could have failed our young players before they even reach a decade of their lives!

The important take-home-message, here, is that our children need to live more active lives in order to build their technical and physical skill (making them more efficient). Thanks to today's 'fast paced' and 'safety first' world too many are not developing as required.

# Chapter 7

In the following chapter we will discuss what can be done to help develop more talented and skilful footballers in their golden years of development.

# 8

# The Golden Years

*"With the young players we work 95-100% on technical skill development. We create an environment for kids to learn new things."*
René Meulensteen – Manchester United First Team Coach.

## Developing skilful players

As we saw in Part I, England has produced players with real creativity; players such as Glenn Hoddle, Chris Waddle, and Paul Scholes. Yet, as a nation, we dismissed what they could do and underused their talents. These players were put into rigid formations which hampered and reduced their skill and expression.

More contemporaneously, many will argue that England has excellent technical players. This is true. England produces some excellent technicians; watch Steven Gerrard, Wayne Rooney and David Beckham cross the ball or play a 60 yard pass with almost missile like precision. They are excellent technicians. But, they are also products of the English culture: the direct style of play which promoted long balls, crosses, long shots, defensive headers, and strong crunching tackles.

There are few, if any, English players who can rival the style of players like Lionel Messi, Cristiano Ronaldo, or Ronaldinho. For too many young footballers England's youth developers have failed to produce players who can *beat an opponent* with world class dribbling skills and creativity.

As we saw in the previous chapter, these top players were not 'born' with these skills; they were nurtured and developed over time. When we think of skill development in terms of neurophysiology then we can begin to understand why we fail to develop the right numbers of skilful and creative players. Simply, our young players are not practicing the right kind of skills to become top footballers and the past 50 years of FA coaching and methodology has neglected skill for physicality and functionality.

# Learning from the streets

Many of the top players in football history have developed and honed their skills on the 'streets'. Pelé, Maradona, George Best and Ronaldinho were all players who spent endless hours playing football, on the roads, as young children. These hours enabled these individuals to hone their skills, improve their awareness and vision, and enhance their dribbling.

The 'streets' are a place to learn and develop skills and the best would excel in these environments. They found and exploited tight areas and attacked with speed and skill. Skills such as one versus one, dribbling, and combination play were all developed. No wonder these players became who they were.

The English side which won the 1966 World Cup developed their skills through 'street soccer'. In the past, football was not what it is today; young children did not have the extensive coaching schools and centres of the present. Kids would play on the streets, away from the eyes of parents, and away from 'coaches'.

The streets would deliver the 'deliberate practice' which is needed to excel. Street soccer allows variation, with different opponents, different sized teams and different ages. Imagine when young kids play against older ones, the challenge they have, the 'stretching' they need - in order to compete. After a while they become faster and more skilful because they are being challenged and pushed.

There were no coaches telling players what to do so they had to make decisions for themselves. It was the perfect environment to develop skilful, intelligent players. And not only this, 'street soccer' developed social skills too; confidence, leadership, expression, friendship and, importantly, competitiveness.

These children were playing in an environment which fostered progression through constant play and the refining of skills. And, of course, when these players played more orthodox matches they transferred their skills with relative ease and looked like 'naturals'. It was not 'natural' talent but practice which produced these players.

Many coaches and ex-professionals in England argue for the return of 'street soccer', where kids can play in the streets or the parks on their own. All this could happen without coaches, without organisation, yet health and safety concerns - and the fear of allowing kids to go out by themselves - have led to an overprotective mindset. The worry for England's future is that many believe 'street soccer' may be dead.

So, if street soccer is too difficult to make happen in the modern age – what else can be done? If you go to countries like Spain, Brazil and Portugal you see small football 'cages' set up all over town - full of kids playing football all day and night. It is here where the players of the future are being developed. Admittedly, the weather and climate plays a part in increasing practice time in these other countries, but there is a clear lack of facilities in England which prevent young children playing these kinds of small sided games. Well, this is not exactly true, there are many five-a-side venues across the country - yet they are often extortionately priced and some have age restrictions.

If there is no way for young players to gain valuable experience during their golden years then the opportunity for developing world class players becomes slim. If the 'death' of street soccer is true, there must be a replacement.

> *"If we want imaginative, quick thinking, skilful players then we must provide the means to produce them."*
> John Cartwright.

# Performing in small spaces

*"Great players don't come from the beach, they come from the futsal court,"*
Dr Emilio Miranda - Professor of Soccer at University of Sao Paolo.

In *The Talent Code*, Dan Coyle travelled to Brazil to see why Brazil produces so many talented and skilful players. He found that since the 1950's Brazil has been practicing with a particular tool that has accelerated the development of football skills and ball handling faster than anywhere else in the world.

He wrote, "The young players of Brazil trained not on vast expanses of field but on basketball court sized patches of concrete, wooden floor and dirt." They played a game called futsal, a game of football played at "blinding speed" which "consisted of quick passes, 1v1 battles, end to end action."

Futsal is a lot quicker, tougher and more skilful than a normal game of football. As Adam Deacon wrote in an article for *Backpage Football*, "The rules set the scene for a battle of technical ability and craft, the lack of space means that players have to be intelligent with possession, which encourages dribbling round the opposition or promotes the player to envision a creative pass they wouldn't usually play in any average game of football." As Robinho, one of Brazil's most skilful players, said, "You don't have time to think, you are tightly marked and you develop a sense for performing in small spaces."

> A lack of space means that players have to be intelligent with possession, which encourages dribbling and combination play with speed and creativity.

The best footballers in the world, Messi and Ronaldo, recognise how futsal has contributed to making them the well-rounded players they are today. As Messi says, "As a little boy in Argentina, I played futsal on the streets and for my club. It was tremendous fun, and it really helped me become who I am."

The game is growing worldwide which is unsurprising given its positive influence on football. More countries than ever are playing the sport, with FIFA describing it as, "the fastest growing indoor sport in the world."

And if you wonder why Spain has become one of the world's best developers of talent then perhaps the introduction of futsal can be attributed, in part, to their present day 'technical excellence'.

Spain's recent success and clear technical mastery of the ball are not unsurprising when you consider the impact of futsal on the nation. The professional futsal league was formed in 1989, which is significant when we consider Spain's emergence in the past decade as a country capable of producing technically accomplished players.

There is a clear link between futsal and the development of world class players. Spain's all-time international top scorer, David Villa, played until the age of nine, and said, "Futsal is a bit more technical than football. I also think that because you play a shorter amount of time, there are different physical requirements, because you need to run constantly." In Spain futsal has become *the* environment for young players to develop and hone their skills.

Futsal helps to develop creativity in players perhaps more than any other version of small sided football. By its nature it promotes imagination, inventiveness and skill, and also improves decision making and spatial awareness. It promotes players to learn and cope in tight spaces under pressure, a significant issue which many English players struggle with.

It would be unfair to blame the players, it is not their fault - they are simply the products of the environments they have developed in. You can see why England develops skills like those of Gerrard and Beckham. Because of the style of coaching and the landscape afforded to many young players, practice conditions have come about that focus on direct play. Basically these practice environments have stimulated the skills of long passing and neglected the ability to master short passing, 1v1 situations, and handling the ball under pressure.

> If England wishes to develop players with the skills needed
> to compete with their foreign counterparts -
> perhaps futsal is the answer.

When we consider the neglect and dismissal of 'skill' in the past several decades by Charles Hughes and the FA, it is really not surprising that the kinds of methods which seek to develop to 'skilful' and 'creative' players are near enough ignored.

Recently the FA have recognised the role that futsal can play, and are determined to change the mentality on it. The National Futsal League has been developed as well as the Youth Futsal Festival, Under 18's Futsal Championships, and a few other projects. Millions of pounds have been invested in the sport in England and with the opening of new indoor clubs across the country anticipated - the future appears bright(er).

However 'organised' activity will not bring about the environment of 'street soccer' and until young players are given the freedom and facilities to simply 'play' then their development suffer.

# Teaching the skills

John Wooden, one of the greatest coaches sport has seen, said this about skill development, "If you don't have the time to do it right, when will you have the time to do it over?"

We have seen that it is almost essential that children develop the necessary skills and movements between the ages of 5 and 11 in order to enhance their skill circuits and make them more fluent and efficient. Practice and activity are the key drivers. And in the previous section we discussed futsal and how important it can be for the development of skill in young players. It is seen by many as the modern version of 'street soccer'.

Yet there is a problem. If we simply allow young players to learn and refine their skills 'on their own', they may begin to develop bad habits in terms of technique and execution.

Although 'street soccer' enables practice and expression, is the associated learning, and mastery of skills, key for the development of good technique? Do young footballers need to be taught to master technique early in their football careers? The answer to this would appear to be yes. As John Cartwright has written, "Footballers need to be taught the game properly. I do not believe that players are born footballers."

Dan Coyle is in agreement too; habits are hard to break and if a young footballer has been practicing the 'wrong' technique, it will be very difficult to 'unlearn' it. Therefore the 'teaching' of skill is important for a young player's future development.

> Poor skill execution and poor running technique
> can lead to increased injuries or restrict the
> speed of a player with (and without) the ball.

The path to 10,000 hours is rarely because of the individual alone, and as Anders Ericsson argues - never 'fortunate' or 'natural'. The development of expertise comes about in part due to strong support, from an early age, from a parent or coach and has clear implications for the future development of the child.

A common theme across history is that those who become the best in their domain are often people who received invaluable support and guidance when they were young. Therefore the importance of having guidance and coaching at a young age is clear. Tiger Woods and Mozart, whose stories and development are spoken of in great detail in Michael's Howe's book, *Genius Explained,* were both nurtured and coached by their fathers, respectively, when they were four.

Lionel Messi's father was the coach of his side when growing up in Rosario which would have given him the extra training and nurturing of his skills which other players are often denied. He was also given more freedom to express his skills, especially his ability to run with the ball and beat the opposition. The constant practice of these skills can be seen in his performances today. Perhaps Messi would not be the player he is today if his father had not coached his side and fostered these talents.

# A lesson from the Dutch

Here is a question for you. Can we develop a Lionel Messi? Alf Galustian, the co-founder of Coerver Coaching, believes that you can. He is certain that the skills of great players like Messi can be trained and mastered by breaking them down into 'chunks' and teaching them to youngsters. When looking at the importance of practice and the building of skill circuits, this idea does not seem so far-fetched.

The Coerver method of coaching and developing players, particularly young players, is based on the model of skill development created by Wiel Coerver, a Dutch football coach, which is based heavily on teaching technique. Coerver has been called the 'Albert Einstein of football'. Coerver Coaching was created in 1984.

The Coerver method was taken up by Alf Galustian and Charlie Cooke and Coerver Coaching was created. Coerver believed that the building blocks for successful players rest on the foundation of individual 'skill on the ball' and that players who don't possess skill on the ball will also suffer with other aspects such as mental and physical strength, and tactical knowledge.

At the core of what Coerver players are taught is ball mastery, which then leads onto improving first touch, striking the ball, running with the ball, and 1 v 1 situations. Players like Arjen Robben have come from the Coerver School of skill development. The Coerver method seeks to break down skills into core elements - a 'chunking' of skills. Through repetition, players improve and refine their technique, eventually performing the skill with greater speed and complexity.

> Practice should be about breaking down moves,
> mastering them, and then perfecting them
> into one fluid motion.

As well as dividing moves and skills into chunks, a key factor in the development of skills is to go slow. By going slowly a player and coach can learn and teach the specific movement (and sequence) which allows for better learning and execution.

In English football coaching there is often a common problem of too much too fast - with coaches seeking to get through as much as possible in a short space of time. Research from Williams & Hodges (2005) has shown that learning slowly, with more precision, enables better execution and longer term skill retention.

Incorporating the player into the learning process, teaching them the sequence and breaking it down, enables the player to become a problem solver for their own skill development. In effect they are able to analyse their own performance and generate their own fixes.

Chunking enable a deeper knowledge of movements to be gained and provide a player with a detailed conceptual understanding that allows them to control and adapt their performance.

## Manchester's technical investment

If you're still not convinced, then allow Manchester United and Alex Ferguson to prove the benefits of the Coerver method of skill development. Alex Ferguson was one of the great managers in football history and has been a key part in the development of numerous excellent teams and players. So when he decided that

Manchester United's academy needed to be modernised and improved, he chose to bring in one of the best technical skill coaches in the world.

René Meulensteen is a name which has become better known in recent years, yet it was twelve years ago when he was first recruited by Ferguson to introduce the Coerver method of skill development at Carrington, Manchester United's academy training ground.

Although it seemed that many academies had ignored much of Howard Wilkinson's Charter in 1997, England's top club and one of the best managers were not as dismissive of the belief that England needed to develop players with more *technical excellence*. Meulensteen was given the remit to overhaul Manchester United's academy system and as skill development coach he was instructed to improve the technical foundation of players and improve their skills, dribbling, and confidence to beat players 1v1.

Meulensteen, who has moved on to first team coach, was brought in, initially, to improve the quality of coaching during those early 'golden years' in a player's life. A coach brought up on the philosophies of Wiel Coerver – he was the ideal man to develop the skills of United's young players.

The Coerver coach changed United's coaching syllabus, concentrating on the technical side of the game, specifically the coaching of 'tricks and moves' which, Meulensteen believes, represent the difference between a good player and great player. Perhaps the most important change which Meulensteen introduced was the implementation of 4v4 matches for players under 10 years of age. As Raymond Verheijen argues in his book, *Conditioning for Soccer,* 4v4 games enable players to become more involved and increase their contact with the ball. More touches of the ball develop the skills which are required for top level football.

Verheijen argues that "Children have only a small chance of mastering the game and developing skills in games," when playing in larger sided games. Principally the players are not involved enough and this does "not favour a child's learning process." Coerver Coaching and the Dutch Football Association have seen the value and importance in these 4v4 games yet Manchester United are the only academy to use this format. Every other academy in England plays competitive fixtures of eight-a-side or more.

After ten years of laying down the foundation for a new way of developing players, Manchester United are showing that development takes time and patience yet the rewards are remarkably handsome. Meulensteen's work has seen Manchester United's Academy become the benchmark for youth development in England.

# Why aren't other clubs learning from the Dutch?

When we watch Spain we see how great their technical skills are, and these skills stem from the coaching of players at a young age. It is no surprise that Barcelona's quality with the ball has come from the introduction of the Dutch method of skill development from previous manager Rinus Michels and Johan Cruyff, as well as a culture of futsal.

The concern about the lack of technical quality which England's young players possess prompted Richard Lewis, who was the executive chairman of the Rugby Football League and chair of Sport England between 2002 and 2012, to compile a report on the state of youth development in England. Lewis recommended that although the academy format should be maintained, English football needed to change their approach to youth development for 5 to 11-year-olds.

Lewis recommended a change in ethos, for the age group, so that much more emphasis is given to skill development and acquisition rather than on results in matches. Lewis recommended that professional clubs must spend more time, with 5 to 11-year-olds, concentrating on 'technique rather than results'. Not surprisingly this is the same advice which Howard Wilkinson had offered in his Charter of 1997. Lewis' report influenced the developers of the EPPP who have been keen to promote the coaching of technical skills for academy players between 5 and 11.

> Incredibly, 'technical skill development' is
> something which English academies
> are only now implementing.

# Summary

Technical skill development has developed world class players and teams. Possessing technical excellence is imperative to a game that requires an exquisite touch in tight areas and with limited time. With excellent decision making and a high technical level a player can deal with many situations with poise and composure. When we watch Xavi, Messi, and Iniesta we see players confident with the ball, even under high pressure.

The research is almost unquestionable; an increased focus is needed on those players between 5 and 11 who are in their 'golden years' of learning. By improving the technical skills of these players English football may be in a better position to develop more skilful players who show confidence when handling the ball.

**Chapter 8**

One academy cannot do it all. More academies need to learn from Manchester United and their approach to developing skill in youngsters. If the culture in England shifts towards technical skill development then the future for English football will look much brighter.

It is not just academy football which needs to enhance its technical skills coaching. In the following chapter we will look at what is happening at the grassroots level and how this is affecting the future development of players in England.

# 9

# The Talent Crucifiers

*"In England you teach your kids how to win, in Spain and Portugal they teach their kids how to play."* Jose Mourinho.

## Developing a love for the game

In the previous chapter we looked at the need to develop creative and skilful players from a young age. We saw how clubs like Manchester United are seeing the value in laying the technical foundations in the early stages of a player's career in order to develop players capable of competing in the modern game.

Now not every player is fortunate enough to be at Manchester United between the ages of 5 and 11 years. But should not every child be given the opportunity to develop their skills at a young age? In this chapter we will see that many children are being put in football environments which not only dismiss skill, but destroy it.

Looking back to the work and findings of Anders Ericsson, on the development of expertise, it is interesting to find that interviews with international-level performers in several domains have found that elite performers are nearly always introduced to their future domains of expertise as young children in a *playful manner*. Ericsson found that a key part of young people's development was that they enjoyed it.

It seems obvious, the more you enjoy doing something, the more you will practice. And we have already seen how important practice is for the development of expertise.

If enjoyment is the key to maintaining motivation then, surely, this should be a vital part of the learning process and environment. If you enjoy something, you are more likely to work (hard) towards it. In other words, attitude is a driver of improvement and achievement. If a young player works hard at developing the necessary skills then they will increase their mastery, execution, and fluency. Working hard appears to be the most fundamental thing for a young player; if a player enjoys what they're doing - hard work can be embraced. The question is: are we providing children with enjoyable and hardworking environments?

> The more enjoyment a young person has – the more work
> and time they are often willing to put in.

In the early years of a young child's football 'career' they will play football with their family and friends, at school and perhaps at holiday camps and weekly sessions. These initial years can be the most enjoyable for a young player because they are predominantly provided with experiences which are fun and positive. The term coined for these early years is the 'FUNdamentals' which, as the name suggests, should aim to give young players the learning and development of physical and technical skills while being… ahem… fun!

## Winning at all costs

*"Developing players for the future seemingly comes second to getting good results."* Chris Green

The largest number of youngsters playing football are playing at, what is called, the 'grassroots' level. At this age, and level, football should be a joyful and happy time for a young child, and for some perhaps it is, yet there is a real worry that this pool of talent is being ruined by poor environments.

The truth is that many of our young footballers are being placed in the hands of uneducated coaches, many of whom are not skill 'developers' but skill 'destroyers'.

For all the well-meaning coaches who proclaim their wishes to play good football and promote the use of skill, as soon as these coaches get in the 'heat of the battle' they forget that they are developers of talent and instead focus on the result.

> The major problem holding English football back
> has been the 'win at all costs' mentality.

The mantra of youth football should be that 'performance is more important than the result'. However, go to your local pitch on the weekends and you will see coaches and parents pushing and demanding 'winning'. This mindset, and environment, created by coaches and parents has limited the performances of players in their quest to win a trophy.

How often do we see teams who favour a more direct style to win games? It may help the team 'win' yet it certainly does not help develop footballers to grow skill and confidence with the ball. The worst example of England's culture is when a young player kicks the ball out of play and he receives a rapturous round of applause for 'getting rid of it'. Astonishing.

Richard Lewis' report on youth football in England made the point that, "An over-emphasis on results leads to a climate of fear, something remarked on by many in the system." He added, "I am not advocating the removal of the 'winning ethos', nor the downplaying of the very successful FA Youth Cup or the desire to produce winning England Under-21 teams. However, match results, especially at the youngest levels, are not all-important."

A 'climate of fear'? Lewis is not wrong; look across most grassroots games on the weekend and you will see what Lewis is saying. The grassroots game has become filled with a cowardly attitude where defeat means failure. This approach favours 'functional' play over expansive and creative football and has ultimately led to 'mediocrity'.

After evaluating the FA's beliefs and teachings over the past decades, can we be surprised by what is happening at the grassroots level? Grassroots coaches have learnt from coaching courses which have promoted a certain style of play, and have been watching football which for the most part was 'savage' and 'barbaric'. It has led to a grassroots youth game which is most often devoid of any skill or quality.

What should actually be happening at this level? Players should be developed who possess skill, confidence and creativity. This is more 'successful' than winning matches and trophies. At the grassroots level there are coaches who are more interested in their own success than developing players. Winning games and trophies is their only goal because, for them, success would confirm their abilities as a coach. Unfortunately this mentality leads to a failure in players developing and improving. If put in the right hands, players could go far beyond what these types of coaches offer them. What is needed are coaches who actually put player development at the forefront of their coaching.

The grassroots game offers the potential to increase the pool of talented players yet, in the wrong hands, it also has the ability to destroy talent and turn creative youngsters into safe and functional 'robots'. I know for certain that there are too many bad coaches with no knowledge of how to develop footballers out there. This should worry the FA, parents, and everyone with an interest in youth development across the country.

# Promoting mistakes

English football is not producing players with confidence on the ball, players who can run with the ball, express themselves and beat opponents with skill and craft. We wonder why we don't produce our own magical players. We marvel at the dribbling skills of players like Messi, Ronaldo and Ronaldinho. The reason England is not producing dribblers, or creative players, is because we are telling them from a young age not to!

The 'need to win' has affected both players' enjoyment and development and coaches' mentality to the game. In far too many cases physicality and 'bravery' have become favoured over skill and intelligence, reducing grassroots football to favour players with 'brawn over brains'. When you watch grassroots games you don't see many youngsters enjoying their time on the ball, in fact when you see a ball approach some players it can appear to be one of the most frightening objects that individual has ever seen!

The truth is that too many coaches distrust 'skill', they worry that it may lead to a mistake which could lead to conceding a goal. Instead of seeing the value in trying new things, too many coaches effectively forbid the use of skill in games.

If a player tries to beat a player and they lose the ball, what is the reaction? Is it to encourage them, and help teach them what they could do next time, or is the scream of "Never try that again!" more common? Grassroots football perpetuates a viscous cycle of negativity and failure.

Just observe coach and parent actions when a child loses a ball; screaming, gesticulations, negative reactions. This environment will not help develop a young footballer.

> Mistakes should be viewed as a learning tool, because they are very important for a player's development.

For young players, mistakes happen frequently and sometimes these faults are punished with the opposition scoring. The answer to such occurrences should not be derision and criticism but encouragement, support, and help for the player.

The pressure that coaches have put on players for making mistakes, can produce a feeling of 'letting the team down', which has developed insecurities in young players.

This has led to stagnation for freedom and creativity, as well as taking away that key aspect of enjoyment. Grassroots football on the most part has become a negative environment for young children to develop and play football.

# Targeted, mistake focused practice

When we consider the route necessary to achieve expertise, we start to see how important the early years of development are. Anders Ericsson's research has found that in order to reach a high level of expertise - there are some specific things which need to be sought. He believes that a performer must be in the right environment and have the right mentality in order to excel. He also has found that a performer requires *focus*; they need to be on the edge of their capabilities and to "continually attend, hone and analyse their performance."

Therefore in order for players to develop they require a challenging environment and, of course, they need to make mistakes. The idea of stretching the player beyond their current levels is essential and in doing so, players will make mistakes.

> Mistakes are not crimes; they not an indictment
> of poor performance but a necessary characteristic
> of skill development.

In Chapter Eight we looked at how Manchester United have implemented the Coerver method of skill development to improve the technical qualities of their young academy players. A big part of this method is the use of repetition in order to master skill and moves - the more you practice the more fluent the movement becomes. And what happens during this time, the player make mistakes, many of them. Yet are they lambasted and criticised? Of course not. The players are supported, helped and guided to improve. This is what development and coaching is.

Far too often there are grassroots coaches who carry out sessions which do not push or challenge players. The drills and patterns look very 'nice' and organised yet there are no mistakes, no errors. The players are not challenged or pushed because their coach does not believe that mistakes or errors are positives, simplicity is sought in preference to invention. The results of these environments are the production of functional, simplistic and 'safe' players.

> Without errors there is a serious concern
> that players are not actually learning!

The problem is compounded further because players do not *want* to try new things for fear of criticism and being shouted at if they make an error. The majority of grassroots football coaches have created players who are fearful of making mistakes, as coach anger and intimidation has restricted and destroyed creative players, instead promoting physicality and fight over skill and creativity. Just imagine how many players could have been stars had they *not* been put in this kind of environment.

Promoting mistakes will allow players to learn and practice in a positive way. And much about achieving greatness is overcoming a fear of failure. As we discussed earlier, if the players enjoy what they do, if they have a love for something, and do not fear it - then they will strive to improve and practice further.

> A vicious cycle is produced where players are
> fearful of making mistakes, which results in
> a lack of development and improvement.

## Creating the right environment

A young player has many different motivations for playing football; they may want to become a professional, they may enjoy playing with their friends, or they may play because their parents want them to. Yet their motivation and willingness to continue to play must be developed through the environment they play in.

The best environment for a young player is one which offers enthusiasm, enjoyment and which, importantly, allows for expression and creativity without the fear of being reprimanded if a mistake is made. If this kind of culture and environment is not introduced across the grassroots game then England will continue to suffer from a lack of creative and technically confident players.

> Creating the right environment is one of the most
> importance roles that a coach has. The environment is
> hugely significant for the future development
> of a young footballer.

How can a coach create the right learning environment for his players? If 'street soccer' has, in fact, gone - then training sessions must give the players a similar education; more freedom to express and learn, and more autonomy. Having a coach who understands this, who knows what to do, and knows how to communicate to players is a necessity.

Young players need to be challenged and put into situations which test them and force them to solve problems. Ultimately this is what football is about. It is essential, therefore, that practice conditions and environments should be challenging.

If coaches develop player skill through realistic game situations then players will be able to make better decisions when it comes to actual games. Isolated practice is, on the whole, ineffective because players have not practiced under pressure situations or been faced with match realistic problems. The development of football intelligence is perhaps *the most* important aspect of football and youth development.

> The best players are those who can solve problems
> and make good decisions, yet these attributes
> are not natural, they are developed.

# Communication skills

The best coaches are those who understand that mistakes and errors happen and who actively seek to challenge players in order to test and further them. The test for these coaches is to spot a mistake and give the player the correct feedback in order to help them improve the execution and effectiveness of whatever they are attempting.

There is a major difference between a senior level coach and an Under-8 coach. Both may have lots of knowledge of the game but if they do not know what motivates and excites *their* players - they will struggle to put relevant information across. At junior levels, one often sees the problem of coaches treating their young players like adults. This is harmful for their development and enjoyment.

> Knowing *what* to say and, equally importantly,
> *when* to say it, are key factors for effective coaching.

The hardest thing for a coach is to stand back and allow his players to simply play, yet this is central to player development. Too many coaches produce an environment where they stop the practice and games too often; they appear obsessed with getting their message across, keen to impress their players with their 'knowledge'.

This failing comes from the FA coaching courses which instruct coaches to intrude with "Stop-Stand-Still" interventions and to constantly 'coach' the players. However, constantly stopping the flow of any game is both frustrating for the players and wastes ball contact time.

Good coaches say little and bad coaches say too much. Creating an environment where players are active, in contact with the ball, and are involved with games which involve decision making in game realistic situations - will be more beneficial for a young player than listening to a coach telling them all he knows for five minutes at a time.

Unfortunately there are too many coaches and clubs who are conducting sessions in negative environments. Let's look at some examples of these coaching environments.

# The Boot Camp

Far too often grassroots coaches conduct 'boot camp' type sessions. These involve intense running, sprinting and endurance work (with no ball in sight). Many coaches believe that long endurance running, often over ten minutes, is beneficial to their players. Yet these players are attending 'football' training and expecting to see a football at some point. As you can imagine this kind of environment does not help players develop their football skills because they hardly ever touch the ball.

As well as endurance, many coaches love to use 'shuttle runs' to work on speed. Again this is not beneficial to young children because it is denying them the chance to work on the fundamentals. There are many *football related* games which include speed, with and without the ball, which are far more enjoyable, active and relevant than the shuttle run relay.

These 'fitness' drills are not helpful to the players' development; fitness can actually be developed more through high intensity warm up activities and games, and in small sided games.

Perhaps the most amazing sight at boot camp is how long a player actually uses a ball in a session. Often the coach has 12-16 footballs yet you only ever see one or two balls in action. Instead of allowing every player at the start of a session to have a ball, coaches restrict them to limited amounts of time in contact with the thing which they came to training to use!

Do these coaches not realise that more contact with the ball will allow more touches, more practice and more development? It will also generate greater enjoyment because, instead of long periods without the ball, the players are actually working with the ball.

It is clear that too many grassroots coaches are guilty of using inappropriate activities – activities which are more suited to adult football than kids' football. Why do coaches do this? *Because they are not educated appropriately in the development of young players*. They are using drills and practices which they have 'seen' adults do or which they have experienced. Yet children are not small adults, they are very different in terms of their physiological and neural development.

The use of simplistic practices which often involve limited or no opposition, or simple 'patterns' which do not force players to make decisions may look 'nice' but they are not helping player development. Too many players end up standing in long lines waiting to take their shot after playing a one-two with their coach. Do you ever look at these players and think how bored they look?

One of the most worrying things is the issue of coaches joining in the sessions (and even matches) at the end. These are young children coaches are playing with; as well taking the most touches, tackling and generally dominating a game - which they should have played no part in - they are putting these young children's safety at risk. This lack of consideration to the potential damage being caused is worrying. It comes down to a lack of education once again.

Now, of course, there is some great work going on at grassroots level and it is not all 'bad'. For many young players grassroots football can be an excellent experience if placed in the hands of a positive coach who allows players to learn and develop their skills, whose positive manner, values and coaching enriches the player's skills and behaviour. For some, grassroots football is an excellent place to be.

Yet the truth is that this is the exception rather than the norm. From personal experience - and many anecdotes from parents and other coaches - there are simply too many poor and uneducated coaches who are working with large numbers of young footballers. This needs to change.

# A need for experts

Although there are some hugely enthusiastic and well-meaning coaches out there, the lack of knowledge of player development and coaching in terms of organisation, planning, and communication is worrying for the development of a larger pool of talented players in the grassroots game.

Overall the quality of coaching at grassroots level, at this time, borders on the abysmal. For all the well-meaning volunteers, there is no doubt that, as a nation, we are destroying many potential stars by putting their futures in the hands of amateurs.

As we saw earlier, the new EPPP plans seek to improve the quality of coaching for academy players, yet we should also be looking to improve all youth coaching. If the FA and Premier League are serious about developing more quality players then surely having more quality coaches working at the grassroots is the way forward?

In schools we would not allow an 'enthusiastic' volunteer to teach our children English, Maths or Science just because they watch documentaries and have some 'experience' in that subject? We want experts who can teach our children and give them the necessary tools to improve in the future. We want teachers who can make the educational process both enjoyable and informative. We would never allow a non-expert to teach our children in schools, so why do we allow it with sports?

The undervaluing of sports in England, especially when compared to other nations like Holland, Spain and Germany has made the mentality towards 'coaching' too casual. Effectively the only requisite is a clean criminal record. Coaching qualifications and experience are not really deemed necessary requirements. In England, it appears that 'anyone' who watches or plays football can be a coach.

The role of the coach is to support, develop and help their players by observing and refining the individual skill of each player. With more understanding of skill development a talented coach can give the correct feedback to help players improve execution and fluency. It is clear that not just anyone can be a coach. Every young player in grassroots football deserves every chance to succeed and should be fortunate to experience good coaching in a positive learning environment.

Youth coaching should not be seen as a volunteer activity but an important and essential part of building the foundation of our next generation. Therefore the FA should be looking to put more qualified coaches to work, at this level, with these young footballers.

> If we are serious about improving our future generations then we need to address the issue of coaching for players in their 'golden years'.

## The FA's role in improving standards

Based on what we have seen so far you would assume that the best coaches should be working with youngsters. Yet, again and again, you find these are the least qualified coaches. The majority of 'quality' coaches, those holding the highest coaching qualifications, are working with older teenagers and senior players.

So, why are we allowing uneducated coaches to work with the most important age group? As with anything it comes down to money. There is a clear lack of proper rewards that coaches receive at this age group. In English football the money is at the top and it trickles down. This has meant that talented coaches seek to work higher up the ladder in terms of age groups because that is where the money is.

> If money is the issue then it is essential that this is changed.
> More value needs to be put on the coaches
> of younger players.

Youth development is where the FA should be most active. So, what are they doing about it? In September 2008, the FA laid out its four year coaching strategy with the intention of having a stronger impact on youth football. After years of mediocre coaching courses for grassroots coaches the FA and their National Development Manager for Youth Football, Nick Levett, have finally started to introduce key courses which will help produce knowledgeable youth coaches.

The new youth modules are the best thing to come out of the English FA for decades in terms of youth development. They actually educate new coaches on the needs of young players instead of simply giving them drills to go and carry out. They teach coaches *how* to coach and not just *what* to coach. They teach coaches about children's development and how they learn.

And yet there is a problem. The youth modules are not mandatory for coaching players at grassroots level; there are still too many coaches who hold just the Level 1 coaching qualification. And why is this? Well it comes down to cost. The FA needs to reduce the cost of their courses to make them accessible and affordable for many more grassroots coaches. Right now coach education courses are far too expensive and cost restricts the development and understanding of many coaches.

Finance is the biggest issue for the grassroots game. If volunteer coaches wish to enhance and develop their coaching then they need to spend not insignificant money on acquiring qualifications… which is not always possible. These coaches are volunteers, they have jobs and families. Many simply cannot afford to go on these courses. Contributions from their clubs are never easy – many of the clubs are barely surviving themselves. Improved standards require highly qualified coaches; becoming highly qualified requires funding.

Perhaps the FA's new initiative, which is being implemented in the summer of 2013 with the introduction of the FA mentoring scheme, will help improve standards. This will see every charter standard club in England being supported by a qualified FA coach. This means that clubs will now have mentors who can guide and educate their coaches in their development. If implemented well, with the right people and philosophy, it could be a valuable step in the future of youth development for England.

What needs to be done is for the FA to support more coaches and clubs. Working with McDonalds they have helped contribute to the development and training of coaches, and since 2002 they have trained more than 20,000 across the country. This is great but more needs to be done.

Can we trust the FA to invest in the future development of talented youngsters? The FA Skills programme would suggest we cannot. For the past few years Trevor Brooking has been on a crusade to improve the technical development of English children. He believes that higher quality coaching is required for young players. His brainchild was called 'The FA Skills programme' and it was created to give more children the opportunity to receive high quality technical skills coaching.

Brooking believes that if the English FA and their expertly trained coaches could work with more young children, and coach the skills and techniques necessary, then the pool of talented young footballers would increase. This sounds pretty much bang in line with what we have been exploring so far.

The FA Skills programme had the right ideas and beliefs about what was required and they were keen to train and develop expert coaches to work with young players. However, because of funding shortfalls the programme was diluted to levels which, in all honesty, led to a failure to achieve its aims sufficiently.

The FA was unwilling to invest money into the programme and Brooking had to find funding from external sources. It took the supermarket group Tesco to fund the project in order for it to go ahead at all. One has to ask questions of the FA and why they would not invest and show a willingness to support a project which would have the potential to develop more talented players. Perhaps it was the use of the word 'skill' which put them off.

## Summary

This chapter has sought to address some of the underlying reasons why England is failing to develop and nurture a large quantity of technically skilful players. Poor and uneducated coaches are stamping out creativity and expression from their players in their quest to win trophies, and in doing so jeopardising the future development of English football. Because of the problems at this level, England's pool of talent is limited. How we develop talent at a young age is fundamental to England's future.

A win at all costs mentality is ruining players and destroying lots of potential players. Competitiveness should not be disregarded but should be managed correctly. Winning should not be the pinnacle, success should be viewed through the quality of the performance. A team and individual can 'win' even when the result goes against them because they are focused on performance and development.

A positive learning environment promoting mistakes, learning, hard work and creativity is imperative for the development of England's future generation not just for football – but for life.

The governing body needs to see their role in the grassroots game as their key interest and they ultimately need to invest and do more to improve quality here.

If we are serious about developing more talented individuals then we cannot blame just the grassroots for where we find ourselves. As the next chapter will discuss, it is not just football skills which young players need to develop, in fact it is essential that young children are developed as well-rounded individuals.

# 10
# Early Specialisation

*"Early specialization is a phenomenon created by self-interested and financially motivated adults"* Mike Boyle.

In the past few chapters we have looked at the golden age of learning, issues with the technical development of young players, and concerns about grassroots football. So far we have focused centrally on football yet, as this chapter will discuss, football is not the only sport a young player needs if they wish to become an elite player. It is not just 'football skills' which young players need to develop - learning different 'physical movements' is even more important.

In turn, it has been found that too much football may be detrimental to the future development of young players. Developing fully rounded players may require less football and more of something else.

> It is the all-round development of young children which is essential for developing footballers for the future.

In the past chapter we discussed the failings of grassroots football yet, as we will see, academies are not much better when it comes to looking after the best interests of young players.

# The dangers of pre-academies

In the world of football academies, where each professional club is desperately searching for that 'special' player, the needs of the player and child are often overlooked in favour of the future benefits of the academy. Because of the poor quality of grassroots football, professional academies started to develop their own 'pre-academy' centres. The argument behind this is similar to what was discussed before: allowing players to work with more educated coaches enables more players to be developed. In theory this sounds like a good idea and yet we have a problem.

Firstly the level of the coaching is not that much better when compared to the volunteer coaches we came across in the last chapter. These coaches are often young lads who possess a level one qualification like their grassroots counterparts. Perhaps their advantage is their ability to perform the skills which they wish the players to perform. However, a lack of knowledge regarding young player development is often evident once again. Furthermore, these 'pre-academies' are failing to understand the *needs* of the young players they are ruthlessly recruiting.

Academies are using the 'failure' of grassroots football as an excuse to recruit 'talented' players at a younger age than the academy rules allow. The *Charter for Quality* allowed clubs to sign players from the age of nine, understanding that taking players any younger would not make sense.

> Academies created a loophole through 'pre-academies'
> which allow them to recruit individuals
> under the age of nine.

The question is: why do they do it? For all the talk of 'developing' players there is a selfish mentality to these pre-academies and the intention of many is to make sure that they don't *lose* a player to another academy.

Although it is near impossible to know if a young child could be the next Wayne Rooney, the fear of missing out on a new Rooney has forced many pre-academies to recruit players with almost a 'scatter gun' approach. They look to bring in as many players as possible and hope to find one or two which stand out.

Yet it makes little sense from a developmental perspective; as Brian Jones, Aston Villa's academy manager highlights, in *Every Boy's Dream*, "Aston Villa spend a fortune looking at boys from six onwards – with the best will in the world I wouldn't know if a six, seven, eight-year-old is going to play in the Premier League in 10 or 12 years' time. It's ludicrous."

At the heart of all this is the competitiveness between clubs. At Arsenal they have an Under-4 group. Why? Because Chelsea have an Under-5 group.

We have a serious problem here. There is little consideration given towards a player's welfare or well-being. In the mind of the young player this is a chance to (most often) play for the team they love, with the dream of being a professional. Yet when the club informs a youngster's parents, a week or two later, that the player is no longer needed, the child is left with a feeling of rejection, which can seriously affect him. Why should this be happening to six or seven-year-olds? It is unnecessary and extremely harmful.

Many coaches express concern at the psychological damage of players being 'rejected' by these pre-academies at a young age – especially for confidence and enjoyment. Surely these academies should take more consideration into how they treat young children?

> It cannot be in a child's best interests to be treated as a commodity - picked up and let go with ease.

# Tommy's story

To highlight this issue let me tell you of the story of Tommy. Tommy is a six-year-old boy who was spotted at a summer football camp by a scout from a local academy. The scout saw a player who can beat players with skill, speed and who can score goals for fun. He feels that he may have spotted some real potential. Tommy's parents are contacted and invited to attend the pre-academy sessions at the club. His parents are very pleased because the scout has told them that he thinks their son is one of the best in the area.

A few weeks later another scout, from another club in the area, spots Tommy and invites him to their pre-academy session on another night. Well this isn't a problem because a young player cannot be signed before they are nine years old and can thus attend as many club sessions as the parents wish for. Tommy's schedule now consists of football training with these pre-academies, a development centre, and his grassroots team which also involves a game for his team on the weekend. Tommy's time is effectively taken up solely with football training.

Because of this selfish approach by pre-academies, to make sure they don't lose Tommy, and his parents' desire for him to become a 'star' player - Tommy is at risk of stunting his development as a footballer and sportsman. Let's examine why.

If we base Tommy's schedule on the 10,000 hour rule then we *could* consider all these 'hours' of football hugely beneficial for Tommy's development. At six years old he is clocking up some serious hours in that quest for the magical 10,000. If it takes ten years or 10,000 hours to reach elite levels then Tommy stands a chance to hit that figure when he reaches 16, giving him a real chance of making it as a pro. Or does it?

Pre-academy coaches will argue that doing more football at a young age gives players like Tommy a 'head start' on the rest, because of the increased practice hours. It has been found that engaging in intense, highly focused, practice and competition can allow young athletes to reach higher levels of performance more quickly than athletes who delay specialisation. Yet there is a paradox to this situation. Too much football at a young age is in fact *detrimental* to the long term development of players.

# Early specialisation

The debate around early specialisation is one of the sternest in sport. Specialisation is defined as 'year-round participation in a single sport, at the exclusion of other sports and activities'. Effectively it involves athletes devoting large amounts of time and effort towards one sport, with a targeted focus on high performance.

It has been found that total early specialisation (like Tommy's schedule) in sports like football or rugby contributes to 'early drop out, early burn out and early retirement from training and competition'.

> Many researchers and coaches are strong
> advocates for delayed specialisation.

According to youth sports expert Brooke De Lench there is no hard scientific evidence that playing a single sport before the age of twelve, or participating in a select sports program at an early age, guarantees future success. As she says, "It has not been consistently demonstrated that early intense training is essential for attaining an elite level in all sports". For De Lench, "Early diversification is more likely to lead to success."

Researchers such as Craig Duncan have found that the benefits of early specialisation are typically short-lived and before too long, the negative consequences of working on a single discipline at an early age, such as injury, begin to emerge.

According to Duncan, who is the head of human performance at Sydney FC, the research literature shows a "significant relationship between early specialisation and injury." He believes that while research into the path of a champion has been used extensively to justify early specialisation, the resulting increase in injury that it produces in later teens has a much more damaging effect on *many more* young performers. As he says, "For every champion that specialised early in football there is 100x the number who were not successful doing exactly the same thing." He argues that it is these individuals who should be studied and highlighted more.

He has also argues that early specialisation restricts the development of the basic motor skills needed to participate in other sports which can lead to long term injury. How many teenage players do you know who have suffered because of injury issues? Osgood-Schlatter (a knee pain injury brought on by overuse while a young player is going through puberty) for example, is a common ailment which afflicts young footballers.

It has been found that high intensity training before physical maturation increases the risk of injury and can delay physical development. Together, restricted motor skill development and a high potential for injury may limit the athlete's opportunities for participation in other sports at a later age, both competitively and recreationally, once their career in their main sport is over.

According to De Lench, young athletes who participate in a wide variety of sports tend to have fewer injuries and play longer, thereby maintaining a higher level of physical activity than those who specialise before puberty. As De Lench adds, "Prior to the mid to late teens, most children are simply not physically mature enough to handle the stress that playing the same sport on a year-round or nearly year-round basis places on their bodies."

In a nutshell, too much sport takes its toll on a child's growing bones, joints, and muscles. It would appear that the surest path to burnout, or an overuse injury, is to play a sport for season after season.

These issues with early specialisation can be seen in the teenage years of those performers who often did too much at a young age. If these persistent injury problems are a major reason why talented teenage footballers don't make it to becoming professional then as a nation we must understand the reasons, address them, and minimise problems.

When we consider little Tommy and how much football he is playing are we not concerned that he will be more susceptible to injuries in his teenage years which could seriously affect his chances of becoming a professional player? Will he also be more prone to struggle with the pressure and expectation heaped upon him at such a young age? As we shall see in the next section it would have been better for him to take part in a multitude of sports in his early years.

# A wide variety

In recent years German football club Borussia Dortmund have enjoyed something of a resurgence in German football. And they have done so by building their success on developing young players. Effectively the club is broke and they realised that in order to achieve anything, developing young players (rather than buying in expensive players) was the answer.

On a visit to Borussia Dortmund's football academy in 2011 their coaches explained what their 'secret' was when developing players. Well, can you guess the first thing they remarked on? It was how 'young' the players in English academies are taken in. Their youth co-ordinator could not believe that players as young as five, six and seven were being selected and moved into the academy system (even if it is called pre-academy). They viewed this in the same way that Brian Jones, Brooke De Lench and Craig Duncan view it: too early and detrimental to the long term success of the child.

At Dortmund they begin to take players in at nine years old, yet they believe that between eleven and thirteen is the best time to bring a player into their academy. The reason? Dortmund want *fully rounded* and developed players and believe that players must have been involved in more than just football in their golden years of learning prior to puberty.

What do I mean by fully rounded players? A study by Fransen *et al.* (2012) found that boys participating in more than one sport before the age of 12 are more physically fit and have better gross motor coordination than those who specialize in a single sport early on.

The researchers tested a total of 735 boys in three age groups (6-8, 8-10, 10-12) for body mass and height, muscular strength and strength endurance, flexibility, speed and agility, cardiovascular endurance, and gross motor coordination. Boys in the 10-12 year age group who played multiple sports performed significantly better on standing broad jumps and tests of gross motor coordination than boys specializing in a single sport.

Spending many hours per week playing different sports was found to have a positive effect on explosive strength and gross motor coordination across all age groups. Job Fransen, lead author, wrote, "When diversifying early, [those] participating in more than one sport, were exposed to a greater number of physical, cognitive, affective, and psycho-social environments than boys participating in one sport only."

> Early diversification means slower progress in the short term (compared to specialisation) - yet is more beneficial for the long term development of individuals.

Based on the report's findings, the authors said it was, "Important that children before the age of 12 years [be] encouraged by their coaches, parents, and other training professionals to participate in sports other than just their 'primary sport', preferably in combination with many hours per week spent in their sports." If children are able to experience other sports such as tennis, badminton, basketball, hockey, handball, and climbing, during the key developmental years between 5 and 11 then it appears those children will be much more rounded than those who focus on just one particular sport. And not just those sports, what about gymnastics and dance which can offer greater agility, flexibility and rhythm? All key aspects in football, no?

# Physical Literacy

It is clear that there is a need to develop fully rounded players who possess different movements: the ability to run fast, slow, change direction, stop, start, turn and twist. By having young children specialise early we are denying them the opportunity to broaden their movement 'vocabulary'. It is this idea of motor skills or 'physical literacy' as it is known, which is important for long term success in a sport like football.

Key physical movement patterns such as walking, running, jumping, hopping, pushing, pulling, bending, twisting, striking, kicking, throwing and catching are all necessary for a young child to develop their physical literacy. It is an extensive list yet children do all these things if they are given the opportunity and environment to develop and learn.

At Dortmund they require teenage players to have excellent physical literacy; they use the term "multi-lateral" development, which is defined as having an ability to have a range of movements which taking part in only one sport, such as football often fails to provide. Having efficient multi-lateral coordination enables both feet or both hands to work together which allows fluid body movements.

It has been found that taking part in football at a young age produces players with specialised movements, which come about from mastering the specific types of movements from playing one sport.

In their book *Periodization,* Bompa and Haff argue that, "Multilateral development, or overall physical development, is a necessity… Multilateral development during the athlete's formative years lays the groundwork for later periods of training when specialization becomes a greater focus of the training plan. If properly implemented, the multilateral training phase will allow the athlete to develop the physiological and psychological basis needed to maximize performance later in his career."

In turn, training versus age should look something like the following:

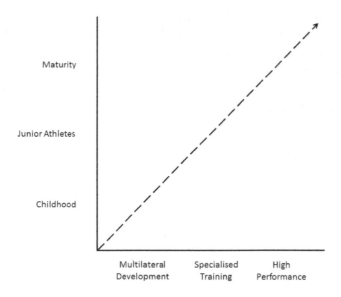

We have referred back to the 10,000 hour rule many times in this book, yet what if we consider those hours to incorporate *not just* football? In the early years of learning, if a child is exposed to a variety of sports and activities then they will have a stronger chance of being more rounded physically, mentally and socially than those who solely take part in football. Yes 'street soccer' and futsal are necessary for players to develop their football skills but, as well as this, what young children require is the repetition and practice of non-specific skills. This is essential because the skills used in most sports are really modifications or adaptations of generic fundamental movements. This is where schools play a major role.

> A young child who experiences early diversification will improve their physical literacy and increase their chances of long term success.

## Schools and their essential role

The physical education curriculum at primary schools is set out to offer broad and balanced athletic provision including games, sports, gymnastics, dance and swimming. Schools are encouraged to offer outdoor pursuits and, importantly, the curriculum is supposed to focus clearly on teaching pupils relevant skills, knowledge and an understanding of physical education. As this section will highlight, many young children in England are being let down by poor standards in primary schools.

When we use the term 'physical education' we see that sport in schools is not just playing and being active but, as the title suggests, 'educational'. When we consider the importance of developing physical literacy it is primary schools which can have the most important role in the development of youngsters. It is here where the foundations for mobility, enthusiasm in sport, and neurological developments are laid.

Research has shown that active lifestyles and taking part in sports improve test scores in other subjects as well as enjoyment levels. Professor Fred Coalter, from the Institute for Sports Research at the University of Stirling, argues that sport contributes to "the promotion and enhancement of education and life-long learning."

And so it was worrying when an Ofsted inspection in 2013 found that some of the content and nature of P.E. lessons in primary schools across England was, as they reported, 'concerning'. The chief inspector Sir Michael Wilshaw highlighted how, "There often wasn't enough physical, strenuous activity in P.E. lessons."

A previous Ofsted report, which found poor levels of P.E. in schools, led to the creation of the Schools Sports Partnership in 2000. £162m of investment was put in place by the previous Labour government and comprised of 675 core staff that ran England's 450 school sports partnerships. Beyond that, the £162m also funded 3,200 school sport co-ordinators, one for every secondary school, and 18,000 primary link teachers, one in each primary school. The role of these experts was to inspire pupils to participate in sport and essentially build the core skills for mobility and health. This gave schools specialist P.E. teachers working across primary schools to add capacity and bring high quality, specialist teaching to children.

However, in 2010 the incoming government misunderstood the importance and impact that sport has on the development of not just elite athletes but the influence that sport can have on young people as a whole. The Education Secretary, Michael Gove, decided to cut the £162m annual funding for the Schools Sport Partnership in England and replace it with a £10m investment in Schools Olympics. It was a decision which would, according to Toby Helm and Anushka Asthana in *The Guardian,* "… threaten most after-school clubs and severely reduce the number of trained P.E. teachers and sports coaches in schools."

The cuts in school sport prompted more than 70 top British athletes, including Olympic heptathlon champion Denise Lewis and world diving champion Tom Daley, to write to David Cameron to highlight how the policy was "ill-conceived." Darren Campbell, a British Olympic gold medallist spoke of the importance of P.E. and the damaging impact of the cuts, "I see the positive impact sport is having, not just in P.E., but across the school curriculum. To cut funding now when such incredible results are being achieved is beyond belief."

> The apparent lack of knowledge from those
> administering P.E. is leading to a reduction
> in young children developing the necessary physical
> movements required for long term success in sport.

Baroness Sue Campbell, chairman of the Youth Sport Trust, argued that the cuts had not only affected the contact hours for children taking part in physical education but it had also reduced the quality of teaching. She said it was, "worrying that fewer primary schools are achieving outstanding marks in P.E. From our own research we know that primary school teachers are not receiving adequate training in how to deliver an effective P.E. experience and this can leave teachers lacking the confidence and competence to deliver the subject effectively."

School sport, particularly in primary school, gives young children a well-rounded physical education which, if done properly, can produce 'multi-lateral' developed individuals. Yet if school sport is failing to deliver the quality and education which it sets out to achieve then our young players are being put at a disadvantage before they even arrive at their first football session. If sporting foundations are not built strongly or correctly then it is hard to conceive that our future generations will be adequately prepared to compete with the rest of the world.

## Summary

In this chapter the importance of early diversification has been promoted as key for the development of fully rounded individuals. In England, however, there are too many coaches, whether in academies or development centres, who are promoting the early specialisation of young footballers, often for selfish or financial reasons. Research has shown that specialising early offers short term benefits yet is potentially dangerous in the long term.

Parents need to offer their children more variety at an early age to develop multi-lateral, core physical skills. Alongside this, primary schools need to improve the delivery of physical education in order to improve the development of their pupils' physical attributes.

The aim of the last few chapters has been to look at the 'golden years' of learning of children between 5 and 11 years. As you can see there is much to consider in order to lay the foundations for future success. We are now going to move on to those teenage years where specialisation in football does become more important.

# 11

# The Key Years

*It's not just a numbers game - it's not about producing mediocre or above average players - it's very much about producing top players and more of them."*
John Peacock, FA Head of Coaching.

So far we have looked at the careers of young players between 5 and 11 years of age and have considered the importance of skill development, improved coaching, and creating positive learning environments which help to develop and improve potential footballers. However, it is between the ages of 12 and 16 where English youth development has really failed to adequately produce players for the professional game.

In this chapter we will consider why academies are not producing the quality of players that nations like Spain, Germany, Holland and France are producing, and consider whether the new EPPP format will aid England's aim to produce a higher number of talented players.

## Academy football

With his *Charter for Quality* Howard Wilkinson took the power of development from schools and county associations and handed it to professional clubs with the establishment of academies. Perhaps Wilkinson did not envisage the issues which these new academies would create, most notably their desire for success at the expense of developing players for the future. Yet he did see that a change was necessary.

**Chapter 11**

When Wilkinson wrote his charter, he did not envision the present academy system of today. There are about 10,000 English players between the ages of 9 and 18 being developed by professional English clubs. Of those 10,000 - only 1% will come through to become professionals. Only 1%!

Wilkinson's decision to give academy ownership to the clubs was not hard to understand. He did not believe that the FA was doing a good enough job with the development of future players (a reason perhaps why Lilleshall was closed down). Yet the move to club development became a case of too many clubs doing their own thing and being left to their own devices. Through a lack of monitoring and evaluation English youth development was nothing but a free-for-all in terms of player recruitment, poaching and coaching (much of which was distinctly average).

The principle aim of Wilkinson's charter was to have 'high quality' academies across the country that developed 'high quality' players. Without question the majority of these academies have failed to produce enough players capable of becoming top level professionals. The truth is that there is a mix of talent and quality between, and within, clubs across the country. If we are aiming to develop a greater number of high quality players then we need to consider what is required for this to happen.

The new EPPP plans aims to create more time for players to play and be coached. It also aims to improve coaching provision, alongside a system of effective measurement and quality assurance. It seeks to keep academies working to a high level. Yet there is an issue in terms of the sheer size of the academy system. Wilkinson's original vision was to have a small group of England's top clubs working with, and developing, England's next generation. But the plan was ruined because almost every club wanted to develop talent.

Brian McClair, who is Manchester United's academy director, believes that the *Charter for Quality* sought to improve two things: provide better coaching and produce better players. He believes that it improved the quality of English coaching, yet he is not so sure that the players have improved. For him "It's been brilliant for the average player. But it's not been elite." As McClair says, "[Wilkinson] looked at the French system and what Howard envisaged was that there would be 10-12 elite academies throughout England. Right away that got diluted. There were about 40 who applied and 40 got the licence."

> There is too much mediocrity across English academies which is why few international class players are being produced.

Many coaches believe that there are too many players in the academy system; 10,000 is too many. The verdict is that English academies are littered with too many mediocre players. Many believe that a 50% reduction is needed to improve the quality of players. Trevor Brooking agrees, "There aren't enough good young players who are elite standard – some clubs will tell you they don't need the numbers of players that they have – and that is where the players and parents get let down."

Why then would academies have players who will simply never become professionals? Well it comes down to the clubs' needs and fears. Each academy requires 16 players for each age group which means they *need* to have players to 'make up the numbers'. The fear aspect comes from the issues highlighted in the previous chapter, bringing in a large number of players at a young age under the fear of 'missing out'.

Aston Villa's academy is a great example of youth development being done right and their methods appear to prove that less is better. The Villa academy has the smallest number of schoolboys in the country and has been like that for a decade. Their rule is that they will 'not sign players just to furnish the team'.

Brian Jones, the academy manager, wanted Aston Villa to be more 'elitist' and decided to merge their 14 and 15-year-old age groups. The intention was simple; they wanted better quality and they knew 60-70% of individuals weren't going to be kept on because they weren't good enough. Villa thus reduced their costs and caused less disappointment among players and parents.

Would a 50% national reduction from 10,000 players down to 5,000 mean less heartache and greater elite development? This is what the *new* EPPP appears to strive for. The new EPPP vision is to create a pyramid pathway where only the best talent moves and plays at the top academies. The new plans seek to address what Wilkinson originally intended, namely to have 10-12 academies across the country, providing the best coaching and facilities, increasing the chances of producing a higher number of professional players.

# A need for a modern philosophy

There is a strong feeling that the governing body for football should provide direction and leadership for the development of young players and coaches; as we know other nations have a clear philosophy and vision of how they want their players to play. The English FA, however, has been hesitant about installing a philosophy of *how* the English game should be. This is perhaps not surprising considering the failures of the past decades and direct style football.

The EPPP has introduced an audit process for English academies that seeks to assess the quality of facilities, coaches and importantly their 'philosophies'. Excellent facilities can be ruined by poor coaching and a limited or non-existent philosophy and over the past year many top clubs have failed to achieve their desired 'category status' because of their inability to prove that their philosophy runs throughout the whole club.

You only have to look at the world's greatest developer of professional footballers, Ajax, to see how important a philosophy and high standards are for developing players capable of becoming elite players. The present manager at Ajax is former player Ronald de Boer who believes that Ajax's youth policy is the right pathway to achieving sustained success. "If you coach and raise up your young talents at a very high level, then you can compete and be a surprise in Europe," de Boer said.

The Ajax style of play, which we discussed earlier with regards to Rinus Michels and Johann Cruyff, has been adopted by Barcelona for over two decades, in which time Barcelona have produced world class teams and players who have been very successful both for club and country.

> At Ajax and Barcelona the idea of a philosophy, a style, has been central to their success, not just for the senior side but throughout all the youth sides.

A club's philosophy is thus essential for the development of future players. Without one how can a club have continuity between their coaches and age groups? Without a vision of what the final product should look like how can coaches of younger teams know what they need to develop and improve? If a club has no philosophy, or vision, of how they want to develop players, a player will have little chance of making it. And if there *is* a vision in place, how much does this idea correspond to the needs of the modern game?

The issue with English academies should not necessarily be that a philosophy runs all the way through but 'what' that philosophy actually is. What is needed for the future success of both clubs and country is to have academies producing players who are capable of succeeding in the present and *future* game.

## Performance over result

*"If we lose, we lose. We need to create players."* Johan Cruyff.

So far we have considered mediocrity in the academy system and a lack of high quality skill. Now, let's look back to the grassroots coaches who were 'killing the creativity' of players and making them fearful of making mistakes. The truth is that the environment in academies is also too intense and critical for players to develop.

A mantra heard from many coaches in academies is that 'performance' matters more than the 'result'. However, in many cases, coaches clearly care more about winning than development and when anyone asks how a team got on in a match - judgement is made on the result not the performance. This is simply wrong. Being competitive is important but the development of players is the key part of academy football.

Dr Andrew Hill, a lecturer in sports and exercise science, in the University of Leeds' School of Biomedical Sciences, has conducted research which has found that some youngsters are showing signs of chronic stress, exhaustion, and disillusionment with academy football at a young age. 167 junior male soccer players in eight academies and centres of excellence attached to English professional clubs were studied and a quarter of the boys reported symptoms of burnout. Players who reported pressure from others, a fear of making mistakes, and other external pressures, were at the greatest risk from burnout.

"What we see among the athletes showing symptoms of burnout is emotional and physical exhaustion, a sense that they are not achieving and a sense of devaluation of the sport. Even though they might originally enjoy their sport and be emotionally invested in it, they eventually become disaffected. Participation can be very stressful," said Hill.

At Barcelona's youth academy, they ask their players, "Did you enjoy it?" As we saw before, enjoyment fuels motivation which makes players want to work harder and practice more. We should learn lessons from the world's best developers and instead of focusing on the result value development, performance and enjoyment. Elite development can still come about with this approach.

Do English coaches see the game in this way? Unfortunately not, results are seen above performance and development, and too many players are asked to fill their specific role and are not allowed to express themselves in case of making errors.

So why do we in England value the result so highly? Les Reed believes the *Charter for Quality* failed because the central concept, a focus on coaching the individual, was compromised immediately with clubs wanting competitive academy leagues. In an interview with the *Daily Mail*, Reed said, "If development coaches are not winning matches they will be questioned about their ability. Then you have a youth team based on results like the first team."

> An environment which understands and allows mistakes to happen, while helping to coach and attending to those errors, should be what academy football is about.

Players, teams and coaches in youth academies should not be judged on results but on how they are performing and developing. A coach's job is to produce players for professional football with players pushed and challenged in their quest to excel and improve. And what is required? Well, mistakes. Yet far too many coaches in academies become irate when they see mistakes. This compounds issues, stunts development, and increases the pressure on players.

## The key years

The most important years for the development of *professional players* come between the ages of 12 and 16. It is here where the most 'talented' players are nurtured in the academies and prepared for professional careers. Between 12 and 16 players should be put through intense technical skill and tactical development. Every player in the academy system should be developed to be comfortable with the ball and have the ability to handle the ball under pressure.

Often, you will witness many English players being rushed in possession or passing without any regard to the needs of the pass. Many passes are 'hit' towards a player with little respect for its suitability or how easy it is for the recipient to receive.

Academy football should be an environment where players are taught to master the ball and develop their all-round skills. An appreciation of the technical elements required such as weight and accuracy of passing, receiving under pressure and the ability to beat players 1v1 should all be taught in detail with real focus.

> Too many players in the 12 to 16 year group
> give the ball away too regularly.

Many players look incapable of dealing with the ball when facing a defender yet rarely do you hear coaches explaining and coaching how to deal with these situations. 1v1 scenarios seem particularly neglected or dismissed in the 12-16 age band. 1v1 situations happen in every game, hundreds of times, and this means that our players should be able to deal with them. However, 1v1 duels are often ignored in academies or are 'coached out' of players. It sounds like grassroots coaching again, doesn't it?

If the modern game requires teams to keep the ball with quality, if England wishes to produce top players and successful teams, then we must learn to appreciate the ball and develop players capable of dealing with 1v1 situations.

# Universal technicians

The modern game requires interchangeable footballers capable of operating wherever required. Arrigo Sacchi, one of Italy's best ever coaches, believes the game of the future will require positional freedom and variability. He believes 'universal players' are the future of the game. We are seeing nations like Spain and Germany developing players of 'the future' who possess all the attributes required for 'universal' football. Yet it is evident that English football is still behind the rest when it comes to developing universal players which may explain, in part, why clubs go abroad in the transfer market so much.

And why does the English system not produce universal players? Pigeon holing players too early in their careers. Players at nine or ten-years-old are being 'labelled' as defenders or forwards and being developed for those specific roles. Yet, at that age, players should be developed to possess all the key characteristics of being a 'footballer'. It is similar to the issue of early specialisation, yet in this respect the issue is specialising a player's position at too early an age.

> Nations such as Germany and Spain are already ahead of the rest in terms of preparing for the future of football.

In England we often hold up attacking players as great examples of having qualities on the ball and, at the same time, neglect or disregard defenders' qualities. This needs to change. England's devaluing of defenders capabilities must be rectified if England is to produce world class players and teams; we need them to be as skilful as forward players. Right now too many lack confidence and quality on the ball which affects the playing quality of their teams.

We cannot speak of players being comfortable with the ball without mentioning goalkeepers who are a vital part of the game. We need to look at keepers as footballers first, and keepers second, because the statistics show that they use their feet 70% of the time in games. This means that keepers need to be as skilful and confident as forwards.

The role of the keeper has evolved to become that of a sweeper and starter of attacks. Therefore they must take a more established role in retaining ball possession and be prepared to receive the ball. Academies should view goalkeepers as part of the team and not isolate them - working on goalkeeping techniques every session. They should be included and developed as part of the team and regarded as footballers first and foremost.

Overall it is vitally important that high levels of individual skill should be available from *all* positions; the more skill available, the greater the playing options available throughout the team.

Imagine if every academy, if every coach that works with players in this country, sought to implement and develop *the technical skills of every player.* If this is neglected in these 'key years' then players will never be good enough to become professionals. And yet we have another problem. Whilst English coaching academies do not necessarily *neglect* technical development - they commonly carry out drills in unopposed environments and fail to develop an essential part of football: game intelligence.

# Developing game intelligence

> *"A high level soccer player is only possible when making constant use of game intelligence."* Horst Wein.

Why is it when we watch Xavi, Silva, and Iniesta play for Spain we see players confident with the ball, even under high pressure? We watch Spain play and ask 'how have they developed such great technicians and decision makers?'

Well, it is simple. It is because these players have been developed to deal with these situations. They are a product of their development pathway and, at this time, their pathway has proven to be very successful and sustainable.

In Chapter Seven we discussed the importance of 'deliberate practice' which Anders Ericsson found to be the key to developing elite performers. Ericsson further believes that professional coaches and teachers play an essential role in guiding future experts to acquire superior performance in a safe and effective manner.

Paul Grech, an excellent football writer, conducted an interview with the man whose book, *Developing Youth Football Players* is the official textbook of The Spanish Football Federation. Horst Wein is a German 'coach of coaches' whose work has influenced thousands of other coaches.

For Wein, what distinguishes the best players from the rest is not good technique and physical preparation, which according to him most players possess, no, what separates the very best players is their level of game intelligence. For Wein this has to be considered the most important ability on the football field. And according to the German coach, young players have to be systematically exposed to games, "which unlock and stimulate their creativity and game intelligence."

Average players make decisions on receipt of the ball, when it is too late. The best players, those who possess game intelligence, are able to 'read the game' and make good decisions as quickly as possible. In doing so, they are able to exploit spaces and opportunities quickly and effectively. Therefore the ability to play in the future is about recognising situations and seeing opportunities early. Before receiving the ball a player should be fully aware of the situation and 'pictures' which are around him. Wein believes that too many coaches treat young players with disrespect by not challenging them and pushing them. He argues that from the earliest ages, "Players must be exposed to game situations in ever-increasing complexity." When we consider the importance of deliberate practice and 'pushing' players then it is clear that what Wein is recommending, and what Spain has developed, is an environment which is challenging and which develops players all round football ability.

In England, a common anxiety is that players are not assured in possession when under pressure from opponents. The reason? They don't practice in these environments enough. Surely it is obvious that players should practice what the game demands of them? Playing games, rather than isolated drills, is a key factor in developing game intelligence. Through games there is a constant change of information and Wein's 'pictures'. Players must be exposed to this and develop their understanding, vision and awareness. The game is the greatest teacher when it comes to developing intelligent, creative players.

Wein believes that players need to be exposed to 'real match situations in training' and that the failure of many coaches to develop intelligent players comes from a direct result of "inadequate coaching training" which too often provides situations "which never happen in a real game" - making it hard for players to develop.

On a trip to Villareal, a professional club in Spain, one coach told me how one training session for the whole academy involved constant small sided games where the players were rotated into different formats and rules every 10-15 minutes. He said that the players never stopped having to make decisions and solve problems and the coaches never stopped the games – only giving information and advice throughout. Doesn't this sound like an environment which promotes learning and development?

> No wonder Spain is producing so many talented players -
> their training environments are perfect for the development
> of skill, speed and game intelligence.

By putting players in progressively tight areas which involve competition – the development of acute footballing decisions is increased. Learning processes are enhanced and the freedom to make errors on a player's journey to becoming a professional enables them to be develop into a master decision maker.

John Cartwright, in his book *Football for the Brave,* believes, "the importance of decision making on time and space in both practicing and playing has been largely ignored by the coaching fraternity." He argues for the same kind of approach to player development as Wein, where players develop "…skills in pressurised practices." He finds it hard, "…to understand how 'drill routines', supposed to improve skill quality, can be used so much when they offer no considerations or decisions on time and space to players."

In turn, he believes that there has been too much of a preoccupation with 'tidy practice' and over-organisation in English coaching. For him this has, "strangled realism, spontaneity and individualism amongst our coaches and players."

# A reason for England's lack of creativity?

Based on Wein and Cartwright's ideas of developing intelligence and creativity we are we starting to see why England struggles to produce creative players. But there is yet another creative issue which England has suffered from… the neglect of the left footed player.

According to the statistics 80% of players are right footed which means that left footed players are a rarity. Yet some of the greatest names to play football were left footed: Maradona, Puskas, Cruyff and Messi, to name but a few. These players were artists, creators, and regarded as some of the best football has seen.

Why has English football never produced a left footed player of this calibre? Well it has to do with how they are developed. In England the left footer is 'rare' and, because of that, they are played on the left side either in defence or on the wing; as we mentioned in part one, the wing means as wide as possible.

When we look at players like Lionel Messi and Arjen Robben, we see left footed players who play on the right, allowing them to come inside and play more centrally. At Ajax they seek left footed players to play in the creative positions of midfield, as they believe that left footed players tend to be more creative. In England, while playing out on the left side, many left footed players are not involved in the game as much as others, and when in possession they will often look to move on the outside of a player.

Imagine if the left footer was placed in the centre of midfield or out on the right. Imagine how much more time on the ball they would have. Imagine what positions they could take up, where they could run with the ball. If a left footer does possess more creativity and expression than right footed players then coaches and academies should be seeking to bring out the best of these players and not pigeon holing them into positions out wide, on the left of the pitch.

It is England's rigid style of football which has limited the development of these key players and which has ultimately stunted their development.

Could we take this advice on-board in our academies and look to develop players for the modern game? In order to meet fluid game situations we need to develop players who understand how and when to change roles and who are able to play in multiple positions. We need academies and coaches who are willing to allow players and their teams to experiment and be creative, away from safe fixed formations and 'results' driven outcomes.

> More imagination, innovation and creativity in coaching and academies will allow player development to flourish much more.

## George Prost's influence

Not everyone in England is developing rigid players who lack intelligence. There is an academy in England which is developing the kinds of players this chapter has been calling for. In the summer of 2012 many people wondered why Arsenal had chosen to spend £15 million on a 17-year-old who had played only League One football. However, Alex Oxlade-Chamberlain has proven his credentials and appears to have the necessary abilities to be a world class player.

Chamberlain was not a one off though; recently the academy at Southampton has produced a number of excellent players who have moved on to play top level football. Players such as Theo Walcott and Gareth Bale, as well as Adam Lallana have all come through in recent years. More recently, players like Luke Shaw and James Ward-Prowse have emerged and proven that Southampton is one of the best developers of talent in England.

Southampton's academy has already provided home-grown talent worth £100 million-plus to Premier League clubs and so it must be asked: what is their secret? Well it comes down to technical skill development and a desire to produce universal players.

The club's relegation in 2005 made it more important than ever to keep developing players through the academy, yet the foundations were being put in place much earlier than 2005. Southampton was amongst the first clubs to adopt an academy system at the end of the 1990s, when they still were a Premier League side. And much of the academy's success can be put down to Rupert Lowe's first spell as chairman. Lowe was a big fan of what Arsene Wenger was doing at Arsenal: the style of play and the philosophy. So much so that he sought to replicate it at Southampton.

> Southampton have been able to appeal to young players because of the structure they have in their academy.

The academy puts a major focus on technical development. In the same way that Manchester United brought in Rene Meulensteen, Southampton went out and hired Georges Prost, a French technical skills coach. Lowe believed that this type of coach was necessary for developing players for the senior team. A lot of the academy's work and ultimate success can be put down to Georges' technical knowledge and detail and his focus on *technique*. Prost works with, and teaches, all the academy players, all the way up to Under-18s.

Like Wenger, Southampton sees the Dutch model of youth development as the best, and has spent over a decade working with players to improve their technical skills and intelligence. While other academies across England favour physicality and out-dated training methods, Southampton are proving that developing intelligent technicians is the key to a successful academy.

Les Reed, head of football development at Southampton, is positive about the club's future, "If we want half our team to come from the academy, which we do, the recruitment needs to be the best, and the development plan for each individual needs to be excellent, as do the facilities, the sports science and the technical quality of the coaching. Aiming to match Barcelona is a big ambition but you need to strive for that to be successful."

# Summary

As this chapter has highlighted, English football needs a change, one which alters the culture of the English game and which addresses the drawbacks of the previous decades. The new EPPP may be the catalyst that improves standards and which moves the level of academy football from mediocre levels to elite - yet it still needs to address what is happening in terms of the level, and philosophy, of the coaching taking place.

English football has the potential to develop world class players, yet the truth is that too many are being wasted by poor methods, styles and coaches. More work is needed to improve technical, tactical and physical aspects in academies in order to develop elite players. As the next chapter will discuss, academies need to do more to develop players' intelligence out of possession.

# 12
# What Academies are Neglecting

*"Don't forget almost 98 percent of the game is played off the ball."* Kevin McGreskin.

## An ignorance of defending

Many of the concerns we have addressed so far have come from a technical perspective in terms of ball handling, possession, and decision making. Yet there is an additional unease that English football is not producing players capable of playing the modern game because academies are neglecting to teach and produce players who can understand and master the 'art of defending'.

In the professional game we now see more organised and intelligent teams when out of possession which means we need to produce intelligent defenders who can deal with such scenarios. 'In game' tactical changes, alongside increased positional fluidity and movement, has made the game much more tactical.

Now, there is a misconception that the term 'defence' means 'defenders' - and those who stick to this idea are most likely to fail to produce high quality players. Defence means what the *team does* when not in possession of the ball, meaning it is a collective effort of the whole team.

Contrary to the English mentality, defending does not always mean running around like a lunatic hunting for the ball; in fact it requires a real intelligence to winning the ball back effectively. Although there are different ways to defend, the key thing, which is often lost on so many coaches, fans, and even managers (it appears), is that defending and attacking are not mutually exclusive. For nations like England the purpose of defending has always been seen as a way not to concede goals, whereas a continental approach to defence is that it is a way to attack.

> If you are not defensively aware and organised then you are not going to be able to compete in the modern game.

Jose Mourinho argues that 'transition', the moment when a team either wins or loses the ball, is the most important part of the game; when you lose the ball, you are most vulnerable, when you win it - you have your best chance to score. The best sides transition quickly and effectively.

Watch Spain when they win or lose the ball and how quickly they make the transition; watch Germany when they win the ball in their own half, in a matter of seconds they are down the other end.

It comes down to the players you have. Spain has developed players suitable for all positions of the pitch who possess high technical skill, speed, agility and intelligence for attack *and* defence. Because of this, the whole side understands their roles and can implement their tactics to perfection. It really is not easy to implement this kind of approach - it takes time, patience, and great coaching.

## The art of defending

What are the reasons for coaches and academies underestimating defending? Well the argument given by some is that players find it boring. This is ridiculous and if players do not wish to learn and master the game then they shouldn't be in academy football. Yet it is also up to coaches to persuade players of the importance of mastering defending. On the other hand, is there an issue with the coaches? Do they find it hard(er) to teach defending?

> Individual and team defending must be regarded as important as possession.

The modern game requires and needs players who are effective both in and out of possession. There is no room for players to not be involved in both attack and defence. It is not difficult to make defending sessions enjoyable as well as informative. Coaches simply need to be more innovative and willing to teach their players all aspects of the game.

Dick Bate is the former elite coaching manager at the FA and has put together a list of what the future defender 'needs' - to make it in the modern game. It is a blueprint for English coaches in their quest to produce professional players.

According to Bate future defenders will need to be 'technically, tactically and athletically better' than they are now. As we have already said they must be great technicians who are capable and confident with the ball. Defensively the future defender needs to be excellent in defending alone in 1v1 situations, as part of a unit, and during transition. They must have the ability to defend while moving backwards and sideways, defending 'feints' and directional changes, defending and recovering when off-balance, being able to press, intercept, and spoil attacks.

A defender needs to be taught the key technical elements of defending: pressing, marking, intercepting, tracking, challenging and heading. They also need to have first-rate decision-making abilities, an understanding of the team's tactics (and the opposition's), and possess leadership and responsibility.

And perhaps the most important aspect for a modern defender is to be tactically aware. They need to have defensive intelligence ('knowing'), and an ability to read and respond to events is paramount. This is most often called 'anticipation' and is perhaps the most important element of being a top defender. Having anticipation means, more or less, knowing what is going to happen next in the game; this includes anticipation of one's own movements, as much as those of the other players..

Normally in England the types of defenders who are memorable are those who make last ditch tackles and clearances. However, making last ditch challenges suggests a poor reading of the game as they see the opposition's attacks late. Surely an effective reader of the game can prevent attacks without having to resort to last ditch challenges?

> It is important that coaches and players are aware of the
> importance, principles, and requirements of how
> to defend individually and as a unit.

Coaches must educate players to understand defending and make their players aware that defending does not mean running around like a crazy person. It is about working smart, not just working hard. Can coaches teach players to mark effectively, to mark a space, or the player, and the reason why? What about distance, balance, the body-shape needed to tackle effectively, and of course the reading of play and anticipation?

> A neglect of teaching young players the art of
> defending will result in one thing – less players
> making it to the professional game.

# Physical development

We have discussed the need to produce technically excellent players and stressed the importance of putting players in more tactical situations to develop their game intelligence. Yet it is important that academies seek to develop *complete* players.

There is a commonly held belief, by many, that academies have become overly focused on the development of strength and endurance between the ages of 12 and 16. Although players are judged and recruited on their athleticism and speed the truth is that not enough academies are doing a good enough job of developing the other key physical aspects needed for players to become professional players.

Above, Dick Bate states the necessity for the modern player to be an excellent athlete. He calls the development of physical attributes the "athletic mix" and believes that every player should have the right mix if they wish to become a professional. Speed development is essential for the modern player and more academies need to improve their players' bio-mechanics and explosiveness.

As well as this, there is also a distinct lack of flexibility training, although some academies have started to introduce yoga programmes in order to develop player flexibility and agility as well as coordination and balance. Yoga and Pilates have been proven to reduce injuries and are thus seen as preventative exercises for players.

> Are enough academies working on the physical
> development of players to help them
> develop skills for 21st century football?

During academy years many players will suffer from growth spurts as their bodies mature. Flexibility training helps with these physiological changes as they can impact on technical ability and also pose a threat to confidence, self-esteem, and social status.

Physical changes may also lead to overuse injuries which can be debilitating and which are brought on by excessive exercise on specific parts of a player's body. The recommendation is that football academies should reduce the importance they place on high tempo sessions and intensity because of the impact they have on players' bodies. Less intensity and more mastery of skill has been found to develop healthier and more skilful players.

# Individualised training

This chapter has sought to highlight aspects which academies could improve upon to develop better players. Working with the 'best' youth players in England should warrant the best work and opportunities. Without question academies need to provide players with more 'tools' with which to perform and develop.

We have spoken too about the time in which to 'specialise', in terms of sport specific but also position specific. Academies should therefore consider how much time they devote to the individual development of a player and how much is 'team' based work. If academies consider their teams as being made up of *individuals* with particular *characteristics* then would their players and teams not improve if the focus was put more on the player, than the team?

'Team based' training develops communication, teamwork, and an understanding of each other (and the game itself) yet there is not enough individual training occurring which seeks to improve and perfect the technical-physical deficiencies of individual players. Training is often used to prepare players in the same way regardless of playing position, individual characteristics, or skill level, and few academies are giving *individualised* training sessions. If we wish to develop excellent technicians then we need to consider if the time in which players are in attendance at academies are actually giving players the focus and attention which they need.

> Coaches and academies need to drill down and develop players individually to enhance their specific technical skills.

# Stretching the player

Earlier we read of Anders Ericsson's belief that, in order to attain expertise, a performer must train and learn in an environment of 'deliberate practice'. He argued that this type of learning is not possible without the student's full cooperation and active participation. Ericsson said that students, "need to acquire representations that can support their planning, reasoning, and evaluation of the actual and intended performance" In turn, from the perspective of deliberate practice, "the scarcity of excellent and outstanding performance is primarily attributable to the environmental conditions necessary for its slow emergence, and to the years of deliberate practice required to develop the complex mediating mechanisms that support expertise." By this Ericsson means that too many teachers and coaches are not placing their students or pupils in environments which push, challenge and stretch their skills and brains to achieve another level.

Ericsson has argued that the key challenge for aspiring expert performers is, "to avoid the arrested development associated with automaticity and to acquire cognitive skills to support their continued learning and improvement." His belief is that learners need to be actively engaged in their learning and that they cannot switch off or 'go through the motions'.

A great example of what 'developing the mind' can produce is taking place in Belgium. In the past several years the English Premier League has been infiltrated by Belgian players possessing skill, vision and creativity and these players originate from a nation of just 11 million people. Belgium has become one of the best sources of talent and the reason why may lie behind their methods which develop the brain.

Ten years ago the Belgian FA decided to improve their standards of youth development. Introducing and implementing their 'philosophy' they sought to produce technically strong and intelligent players who could improve the standards of the national side and enable Belgium's top club sides to compete with the financial might of Europe's elite.

The Belgian FA, as well as clubs like Anderlecht, Standard Liege and Genk, sought to develop a 'style' of play, most commonly a 4-3-3, and sought to develop attacking sides with technically excellent players.  In a presentation on Belgium's youth development, Bob Browaeys, who is the Under-17 national team coach, covered the important factors which have helped Belgium produce so many talented players in recent years.

Their philosophy was heavily centralised around the *player*. In their opinion it is important to let the player make their own decisions, to experience the game and develop in their own way. This idea of support but not instruction is important for the development of intelligent players and gives players confidence. The job of the coach is to help the players make the right decisions, to find a solution to problems, and to do it with positive coaching.

Browaeys also spoke of Belgium's 'zone philosophy'. They need intelligent players who understand what they are doing. Browaeys' argument for this method was that a 'zone philosophy' aids the reading of game situations, the process of 'decision making', the courage to take initiatives, the ability to communicate, as well as aiding concentration. Factors such as perception and attentional focus are central to developing the intelligence which we have covered already. As Browaeys says, "It is important to put brains in muscles."

This is where we introduce Michel Bruyninckx and a new phenomenon which is changing the way academies will view player development; it's called 'brain plasticity'. Bruyninckx is Standard Liège's academy director and in an article by John

Sinnott, in *The Blizzard*, he points out that top level performance requires high concentration and creativeness, which is only possible if you bring the brain into a conscious process of performing. When describing what's wrong with today's youth development Michel Bruyninckx points to his head. "We need to stop thinking football is only a matter of the body, skilfulness will only grow if we better understand the mental part of developing a player. Cognitive readiness, improved perception, better mastering of time and space in combination with perfect motor functioning."

The idea behind his approach is simple: to make players think as quickly with their brains as they kick the ball with their feet. "We need to develop an engram - a neurological track - in the brain," said Bruyninckx, who aims for his players to be in a state of "conscious" learning at all times when they are training and playing.

> It is about creating new connections in the brain's circuitry and hard wiring them in.

Bruyninckx's approach, which he calls "brain centered learning", involves throwing the student into the pool of the learning experience so that they are fully immersed in the experience.

This kind of challenging environment, similar to what Ericsson believes is essential for elite development, is what Bruyninckx is attempting to produce in all his time with the players. Bruyninckx seeks to enhance the cognitive development of his players by 'never letting them rest'. His training tactics try to force the players' brains to constantly multitask so that in-game decision making can keep up with the pace of the game. "You have to present new activities that players are not used to doing. If you repeat exercises too much the brain thinks it knows the answers," Bruyninckx said. "By constantly challenging the brain and making use of its plasticity you discover a world that you thought was never available. Once the brain picks up the challenge you create new connections and it gives remarkable results."

These methods incorporate the work of Paul Bach-y-Rita who is one of the great pioneers in understanding brain plasticity. In *The Brain that Changes Itself*, the author Norman Doidge follows the work of Bach-y-Rita and discovers that the brain is far more plastic and malleable than previously thought. The work is seen as a revolutionary shift in how the brain and skill development are viewed. Plasticity, or neuroplasticity, describes how experiences *reorganize* neural pathways in the brain.

This idea of 'brain centred' learning is not something every coach in football agrees with, yet there are more and more coming around to the idea of training the mind. And which teams, or nations, have taken these methods on board? Well it is no surprise that Barcelona were one of the first clubs to take Bruyninckx's methods seriously. Since then Bruyninckx has met with one of the world's best coaches in Jose Mourinho, and (as mentioned above) has been made Standard Liege's academy director.

# Summary

There is no doubt that today's coach needs to innovate and get creative in order to produce players who have the capabilities to play in the modern game. Academies in England need to put higher demands on their coaches and players in order to allow both to reach new levels of excellence.

The time of accepting mediocrity must end and the striving for excellence must begin. Coaches need to be people who are able to do new things and inject new ideas into the game, rather than blindly repeating what previous generations did before them.

Could England's neglect or distrust of master defending, speed development, and the mind be parts of the problem which is holding back English youth development?

Coaches need to put their players in situations and environments which are challenging and complex and which require players to actively focus on their development. Without this a player will not learn and improve most effectively. Furthermore, the idea of 'cognitive development' needs to be embraced more by English academes and coaches.

As this chapter has addressed, modern coaches need to be excellent teachers of the game in all areas. Academies should be making sure they have 'specialists' who can provide their players with world class learning environments - which are constantly challenging. The key to England's future will come from coaching.

# 13

# Many Great Trainers,
# yet Few Teachers

*"Coaching is about the skill in how to educate your players. It is knowledge that is invaluable and the ability to pass it on."* Clive Woodward.

## Quantity or quality?

England suffers from a distinct lack of coaches. The statistics confirm this. For many this is the single biggest reason why England is failing to produce a higher number of quality players. Compared to other countries England *simply* does not have enough coaches *with* top qualifications.

Look at the difference here between England, Germany and Spain when it comes to coaches who hold UEFA A, B, and Pro Licence qualifications; awards which indicate a certain quality in coaching.

| COUNTRY | COACHES |
|---------|---------|
| ENGLAND | 2,769 |
| GERMANY | 23,995 |
| SPAIN | 34,790 |

England has 10% of the number of licensed coaches that Spain and Germany has.

Now, of course, the assumption is that England needs to add 'more' coaches to the system, yet the truth is that it is more *quality* which is required. Quantity is pointless without quality. And as this chapter will discuss, the new academy plans are worthless without great coaches.

## A cultural issue

"Many great trainers, yet few teachers," is a quote from Johan Cruyff who made the point that many coaches in England are very good at motivating, cajoling and putting on sessions with great tempo and energy yet when it comes to actually teaching their players about the game of football, they are very much lacking.

It is hard to disagree with Cruyff in his assessment, especially when we base the English coaching methods on the Charles Hughes philosophy of *up and at 'em* football.

> The national game and traditional coaching methods have promoted high tempo, almost reckless, football. Other nations have proven this method is flawed.

One of the best coaches which England has produced is Steve McLaren and after working in Holland at FC Twente, he saw the problems of the English culture. In an interview with *The Guardian's* Stuart James, McClaren made the point that the Dutch have a different agenda, "Holland is a football nation, a coaching nation. They develop coaches here."

The ex-Manchester United coach identified coaching as an area where England needs to improve most of all, "Everybody here wants to 'get the ball out'; they want to be a coach. They discuss with you not winning or losing, they discuss tactics: 'Why did you play that team? Why did you make that change? What did you say at half-time?' It's not about: 'Win, you're the hero; lose, you're the bum; draw, you're somewhere in between.' And the analysis is good."

And he believes that the young players in the Netherlands and Germany are much more advanced in terms of their "football intelligence", explaining how they know "when and where to find space" from a young age. There is that word again, *intelligence*.

What is important for a player of any age, especially those between the ages of 12 and 16, is that they are educated by qualified forward looking coaches; the unfortunate truth is that too many players in this age bracket are being ruined by bad coaching.

> It is important that football coaching becomes a respected profession for the future of English football.

# A lack of quality

Being a football coach can be one of the most inspirational professions and highly influential for young children and teens. If we seriously want to improve the standards of our young footballers then coaching needs to become a respected profession which rewards the best teachers of the game.

The role of a youth coach is not a trainer but a teacher. Young players need guidance, support, and expert knowledge of how to improve as footballers. Do enough coaches in academies possess the skills needed to play this role? Do they have the ability to bond, to be understanding to players' needs, and to empathise with their feelings and emotions? Can they communicate the right way? Are they compassionate? Can they be positive and challenge their players? These are the characteristics required for youth coaches to develop all round individuals.

From personal experience and stories from other coaches there are too many coaches in these key development environments who are negative and authoritative, and who lack understanding and compassion of the players' needs. This is why many kids between 12 and 16 lose the love of football and do not develop and progress to the next level.

> Many players in academies are working with coaches who still do not understand that their main role is to 'facilitate' player development.

Coaches need to know more about teaching and how adolescent footballers learn. A 'trainer' will work their players hard, but a teacher will develop intelligent footballers who are excellent decision makers. The best coaches are those that know when and what to say at the right time. The hardest challenge for a coach is to sometimes say nothing.

As we saw in the previous chapter, academy training sessions which overuse unopposed practices are not helping players develop their game intelligence. Players are being hampered by basic and unchallenging drills which offer little relevance to the game and which look 'pretty' but which fail to develop players sufficiently. It is a similar situation to that of grassroots coaching where mistakes and failures are deemed 'unacceptable'. Unfortunately, coaches continue to view mistakes as negative instead of an essential part of the learning process.

> Until coaches start to accept mistakes as part of the learning process, how will players develop?

# Guided discovery

The issue with many academy coaches in England is not that they are bad coaches, many have a deep and thorough knowledge of the game itself, but many lack the communication skills required to educate and inspire the players they work with. Too many coaches believe that they have to shout, instruct, and appear to be 'doing' something. The continuous commands and instructions given by most coaches before, during, and after a match, prevent most players from having to think.

According to John Whitmore, in *Coaching for Performance*, a pupil only remembers 19% of what the teacher taught him some three months later through instruction or telling, 32% of what is demonstrated and explained, and 65% when pupils were given the opportunity to generate information on their own with help of the teacher. Therefore young players should be actively participating in the learning process. True learning takes place best when decisions are made by the pupils. Coaches should attempt to limit frequent instructions and solutions.

> Too many coaches are afraid to let the game teach the players. True learning and development takes time and patience.

# A picture paints a thousand words

When considering communication skills we need to discuss the importance of body language. Coaches at all levels need to develop excellent communication skills which incorporate words, tone and body language. Did you know that body language is the most important part of communication? And that tone is more important than the words used? Research by Mehrabian and Wiener (1976) found that body language equates to 58% of communication, tone 35%, and words just 7%. Therefore it is clear that what players see is more important than what they hear.

How many coaches are aware of this? Not many when you observe them in action; their body language is often negative and closed; their tone is often authoritarian and pessimistic even though the words may be positive and helpful. It is clear that if coaches wish to develop their coaching then they must address their communication skills first.

Encouraging and supporting players rather than being critical is essential for developing players. Fear of critical comments from the coach leads to players who give up responsibility and assign criticism to somebody else. This is not helping to develop players for the professional game. Confidence without fear is necessary and coaches have a major role in developing and nurturing this mindset. The importance of communication, verbally and non-verbally, can have a significant impact, both positive and negative, on an individual.

If we wish to develop smarter decision makers on the pitch then coaches really need to create the environment which promotes learning and where communication is not commanding but questioning, where guided discovery is used to unlock a player's mind and help their intelligence to grow. This is real coaching and teaching and this is where England will produce more players for the modern game.

## The attitude and behaviour of the coach

The job of coaches who work with young players is to develop and improve them by giving them the tools and environment with which to learn. The level of coaching in academies needs to be improved without doubt, yet perhaps what is needed above all is the 'willingness to teach'. To have a career coaching football is one of the best jobs to have, perhaps not in terms of pay but certainly as a feeling of satisfaction. Yet you wouldn't think it when you talk to coaches and see them work. Many look disinterested or bored and they then wonder why their players appear to show the same characteristics during the session.

> A teacher needs to inspire their pupils to learn and work hard, to achieve and improve.

The coach's character and personality influences the way his players approach the game, in terms of their mentality and enjoyment. The coach transmits his attitude towards the game and development to his players. Therefore the coach has a huge influence over the players they work with; this is a responsibility which should not be taken lightly.

Although there is some excellent work going on across England's academies the truth is that unless the quality across age groups and academies is higher - the potential of a player can be damaged. If anywhere along a player's trajectory, he has been with a mediocre (or worse) coach, that player's ultimate peak has been negatively impacted upon.

> An environment which promotes learning and which understands mistakes will often produce players who are expressive, adventurous, and creative.

## What matters more? Performance or result?

English academies should be providing stimulating coaching programs in which the player and coach are constantly looking to broaden their knowledge and experience of the game - pushing themselves to new levels. Why are coaches not promoting these environments of player-centred learning? Well, we must return to the 'win at all costs' mentality.

Academies profess to care about performance over result yet still cannot get away from the judgement of results. A competitive environment should be promoted in academies, players should be taught to be 'winners' because this attitude is essential for professional football. However, if trying to win limits player development because they are not allowed to make errors, or try things in games without the risk of being subjected to frustration and anger from the side, then how can we expect progress to be made?

In the last chapter we saw that academy players are under intense pressure and stress which is causing burnout. Whilst the end goal is to deliver professional footballers, when these players are 12, 13 or 14 the focus should be on the 'process goals' to achieve the end goal. Perhaps a greater understanding, empathy, and some realistic expectations that promote short term process goals will benefit the long term development of the footballer.

> Too often the pressure to win is put on players by coaches and parents and expectations are too high at too young an age.

# Tactical development

Rodolfo Borrell joined Liverpool's academy in 2009. He is now the head of academy coaching and has overseen the development of a number of academy players who have made senior appearances for the club. He made a comment, when he arrived at the academy, which highlighted the issues English development has, "The Under-18s had no centre forward, no balance. They had no tactical level, no understanding of the game, we are working hard, but you can't change things overnight."

No tactical understanding of the game? Clearly English football has a long way to go if one of England's best academies has players at Under-18 level who lack the intelligence needed for the game.

For much of the previous chapters our focus has been on 'technical development'. Yet for coaches it should be very hard to separate technical development and tactical development. For instance, if sessions are oriented towards 'game realistic' situations then there will always be a tactical element to the practice.

Tactical development educates and develops the footballer making them a better decision maker on the pitch. Including tactical elements in sessions is paramount. Rafa Benitez believes that "It's important to try to ensure that young players acquire the best technical-tactical toolbox possible so that they can respond to the majority of the many problems they will encounter in the future, with the help of a devoted coach, within a specific model of play."

The best method of developing this 'toolbox' is the game itself. Like we discussed in the past chapter, the training sessions at Villareal were focused on many small sided games which cover all the elements of the game. Are English coaches and academies using these types of environments enough to develop intelligent footballers?

# Developing expert coaches requires expert teachers

*"What's missing in our game is coaching the coaches. We have to coach the coaches better and that will improve the English game and the English player. We have to make them more intelligent."* Steve McLaren.

The thirst for learning and knowledge must be in each coach and academies must strive to modernise their methods for the present and future. Anticipating what the game will be like will be crucial for developing a philosophy which helps develop players. Yet, perhaps, the major aspect which needs to be addressed is the tutoring of future coaches.

Coach education from level one to UEFA's A licence should promote divergent thinking, an ability to express opinion, an understanding of new technical-tactical needs, and the promotion of creativity and innovation. Unfortunately the state of coach education in England is similar to the level of players and coaches... mediocre.

This is not surprising if we consider that coach education is the foundation for everything else. If the foundations aren't high quality it is hard to believe that the structure which is built upon them will be too.

Coach education needs to be of a higher quality in order to develop world class coaches and ultimately world class players. This is where the English FA needs to be held to account.

By far the best coach educator in England is Dick Bate. We came across Dick Bate in Chapter 12, and he is currently the academy manager at Cardiff City after being recruited from the English FA's Elite coaching manager role. His knowledge of the game and his ability to inspire and educate coaches of the future has made him an invaluable resource for many English coaches.

Bate's clinics showcase a knowledge of the technical and tactical needs for the modern player and teams, as well as a deep knowledge of what is required to be a master coach. His belief in the need to be a great communicator is one of his biggest lessons. He implores coaches to saturate themselves in the game and become students of it. Regrettably, only a small number of England's coaches have been fortunate enough to experience and learn from a great tutor like Dick Bate.

The English FA need far more quality coach educators across all levels of the coaching spectrum who can educate and inspire future coaches to deliver high quality coaching to their players.

> If we want better players then we need better coaches and this means great coach educators.

# Summary

Too often in England we have invested in players and facilities but neglected investment in the coaches. These coaches have the future of England's players in their hands – it is a massive responsibility and one they should take real pride in. England's next generation looks to these coaches to make them better players.

Spain invested in coaching 20 years ago and today we see the benefits. Germany did it a decade ago and they are proving the benefits of that in 2013. Coach education - producing master coaches for all levels - is essential.

Yet the worry is that it is a 'lottery' whether players get a positive and progressive coach or a negative 'old school' coach. This gamble is simply not acceptable for the development of future players. Standards need to be raised across the board if England wishes to produce more high quality players.

In the next chapter we will we look at the final step for young players: progression to the senior level. We will see that making youth development a 'success' comes down to the first team managers.

# 14
# Bridging the Gap

*"It might all mean that youth development is no longer seen as a priority and there is already a massive problem with the lack of opportunity given to players of 17 and over. It will impact on the national team if we don't have players coming through from the academies."*
Howard Wilkinson.

## Success or development?

For the past several chapters we have discussed academy football and what is required to develop players. And for all the promise of youth development and improved standards, developing players is the 'easy part', what matters most is integrating them into the first team.

It was reported that Fulham's youth sides have been very successful this past season, yet youth development is not about winning competitions but preparing players for professional football and I cannot recall too many Fulham academy players breaking into the first team.

The issue of youth development and senior football is a tough one. A coach of a professional academy told a story about the manager at a Championship club. He explained that this manager had two choices; firstly he could offer three academy players a professional contract for three years each or secondly he could bring in a player on loan from one of the top Premier League sides. His budget would only allow him to choose one of these options.

He chose to bring in the loan player and released the three academy players. His reasoning for this was that the career of a manager was no longer than 18 months and he would probably not see the benefits of those academy players until after he left. Thus he chose, selfishly, to help keep his job rather than think of the future of the club and the value of the academy.

This story highlights the issues of attempting to 'bridge the gap'; senior football is a results business and many managers do not have long term security which often makes them reluctant to 'risk' youth. How many players' careers are stalling or ending because of this short term view?

> Questions need to be asked as to what the
> intentions of academies really are.

# Development does not stop at 16

English clubs put 10,000 boys aged between 9 and 16 through the academy system, yet only about 1% of those boys become professional footballers. The maths just does not make sense, it is not economical. Clearly there is a problem which money cannot fix. What can the clubs do to improve a player's chance of making it in senior football?

We have discussed the importance of the early years of player development yet, as this chapter will discuss, many players are being let down when they need the *most* support. All the work we have seen between 5 and 16 means little if players are not developed and challenged further between the ages of 17 and 21. Many clubs are neglecting player development at this time which is preventing many from bridging the gap between youth and senior football and thus preventing England from producing more players.

So, why do players not kick on from 17 to 21? One problem is that many clubs are 'judging' their players at the ages of 15 and 16 and not allowing them time on their development path in terms of maturity and physicality, as much as their technical and tactical development.

A common point raised in England is whether players like Xavi, Iniesta or Messi would have been deemed 'too small' at 15 or 16 years old. There is the strong possibility that the majority of teams in England would have viewed them as too lightweight and cut them from their squads. Imagine how many potential creative geniuses have been left behind by the English belief regarding small players.

The issue of physicality is something commonly seen in English academies. Young players, often those regarded as 'late developers', can be left behind by academies who favour physical attributes over technical and tactical intelligence.

Therefore to judge players at 15 or 16, when they are still maturing and developing, appears lunacy. These players still have five to six years of development to go, perhaps even more! If they are pushed out of the system at this age they will no longer have the opportunity to develop further.

If these players were given these extra years to develop surely they would be closer to achieving the expertise associated with 10,000 hours and perhaps judgements could *then* be made about their 'true' ability? Instead academies are too rash in their decisions, too quick to judge, and they end up cutting players in the mid-teens. Why is this? Well it has to do with the clubs' ability to recruit foreign players at 16 years of age.

> If youth development was viewed as a footballer 'developing' until the age of 21, or even 23, like clubs across Europe do, would English sides not produce more talent?

## Foreign talent or clubs which are killing English players?

*"When we set up the academy system, I don't think anyone envisaged it would be filled with anything other than Brits."* Trevor Brooking.

We have already discussed the influx of foreign players coming into the Premier League and how this was depriving English players of development due to lack of playing time. Youth development in the English game has become globalised and multi-national and there are many who believe that this philosophy has affected England's potential to develop world class players. When analysing the top English sides' youth development methods there is certainly a propensity to favour talent over domestic nationality.

This is not to say that English football has not improved because of foreign influences and imports. Imagine what the game would be like without it! As Chelsea's Under-19 coach Dermot Drummy says, "We have learned from the influx of foreign players over the years. Players have learned about technical ability and I think the coaches have learned too. So it is onwards and upwards for the future of English football. It is in a good place."

The particular issue of clubs neglecting academy players occurs when players turn 16. Why is this? Because at 16 years of age England's top clubs like Manchester

United, Liverpool, Chelsea, Manchester City and Arsenal immediately go looking for the best 16-year-old foreign players, because it is at this age that they are allowed to sign them. Other nations do not do this to the extent that English clubs do because *their rules don't allow it* and many clubs outside of England do not have the deep pockets needed to fund this level of signings.

Let us look at Arsenal. When Arsene Wenger arrived in England in 1996 he felt that English players 'lacked the touch, subtlety and tactical intelligence to compete with those around Europe'. He made the decision to bring in young foreign talent to help improve the team (and the club's finances). This mistrust of British qualities reached its peak in February 2005 when Arsenal became the first English club to field an all-foreign 16-man squad in a Premier League fixture at Highbury against Crystal Palace.

Wenger's assessment of English talent cannot be doubted, yet were his actions - to recruit so voraciously from abroad - correct? He saw an opportunity to exploit the system and did so.

As witnessed in Chapter 2 the 'home grown' rule in the Premier League accounts for any player (under the age of 21) from any nationality that has been trained and developed in the country for three years. Cesc Fabregas is a perfect example. This loophole enables foreign players to be classed as home grown and allows teams like Arsenal to field non-English sides in the Premier League. This rule clearly does not benefit the national team at all.

And what about players who arrive at 16 years of age? For the foreign player, being moved to a new country at the age of 16 and being expected to adapt is ethically dubious. For all the Cesc Fabregases of this world, how many of his peers have been ruined by the vicious and soulless pursuit of attempting to uncover 'the next big thing'? Would it not be better if young foreign players were not allowed to move abroad until they were at least 18, more in line with university age, where a player is now a young adult and not an adolescent?

Now professional football is a tough environment and not everyone can make it, yet surely these young foreign players would be better suited learning and developing at home? For the good of these young foreign players, and English players, and ultimately the national side, more needs to be done to prevent English sides poaching young talent from abroad. Aside from helping foreign players develop less abruptly, it will allow more English talent to be given the chance to develop and progress from 15 to 21.

# The hoarding of talent

When Roman Abramovich arrived at Chelsea he created a new superpower in England and across Europe. He sought to buy the best talent around and his goal was clear: to win every trophy possible. With this kind of mentality it is often very hard to integrate young players into a team with such lofty ambitions (especially when your manager is Jose Mourinho who often shows a distrust of youth because they are liable to make errors).

Chelsea's academy is regarded as one of Europe's best, and in terms of facilities and coaching it is, yet what is the point of having a youth academy if you do not attempt to produce players for your first team? If Chelsea's youth development is so impressive then it begs the question as to why there are so few youth academy prospects breaking into the first team.

The problem appears to be an inability, or lack of will, to provide young players with opportunities for the first team. Expectations at Chelsea are viewed in the short term which results in much of their young academy talent being neglected.

In recent years there have only been a few English players coming through the Chelsea system. They include: Josh McEachran, Ryan Bertrand and Nathaniel Chalobah. Bertrand was actually at Gillingham until he was 16 so cannot really be said to be a 'product' of Chelsea unlike McEachran and Chalobah who were at Chelsea since their pre-teens.

McEachran's history highlights Chelsea's inability to integrate youth. When he first came onto the scene he received a lot of attention. Frank Lampard spoke highly of his intelligence and creativity and it appeared that Chelsea had produced a player who could break through into the first team. Yet four years later and he is now on loan at Middlesbrough after experiencing a poor time on loan at Swansea under Brendan Rodgers. For all his potential he has not been given the opportunity to continue his development fully over the last few years, and because of this he has not progressed to the levels expected.

> The truth is that 16 to 21-year-old players will not progress unless they are given the opportunity and experience to play first team football.

The most important aspect of becoming a player at this age is *to play*. Dermot Drummy has demanded that British kids are finally given a proper chance at Stamford Bridge. He has seen young stars such as McEachran and Chalobah sent out on loan and argues that his youngsters cannot keep being blocked by expensive foreign signings. In an interview in *The Mirror* he voiced his concerns and frustration,

"It's difficult because Chelsea will buy ready-made players," said Drummy. "But the bottom line is you've got to produce a player. There is a second tier now, where the lads like Nathaniel and Josh tend to go out on loan. But there has to be a pathway and opportunities, in my opinion, for the young British players to get a chance."

The problem at Chelsea is that because they have an owner who demands immediate success, an owner who is unwilling to be patient and give his managers time to develop and plan for the future, the long term view is often disregarded. And, of course, there is a Director of Football at Chelsea with a large chest of money, and he is happy to spend it on some of the world's brightest young talent… players such as Eden Hazard, Romelu Lukaku, Oscar, and David Luiz. These are exceptional players, no doubt, yet it appears Chelsea has no vision or plan for integrating their academy players into the first team.

If you are a young Chelsea academy player and you see players like Lukaku (bought for £20m) going out on loan then you have to ask yourself how likely it is that *they* will become a Chelsea first team player, let alone *you*. Players like Lewis Baker, who is clearly a talented player, will be wasted by staying at Chelsea. And this is what makes the news of Kasey Palmer, signed by Chelsea in April 2013 from Charlton, all the more worrying.

Chelsea has purchased the 16-year-old Palmer for £200k which could rise to £800k based on appearances. Does Palmer have any chance of making it at Chelsea? The odds are very slim and so surely it would have been better for him to stay at Charlton, where opportunity would be more forthcoming? Could we see another talent ruined by moving to a big club?

> From the outside it looks like Chelsea are simply hoarding players; a process that could ultimately ruin a player's career.

## Bright lights ruin careers

You only to have to look at the stories of John Bostock, Tom Taiwo and Michael Wood. In all instances it was a case of 'too much too young'.

John Bostock appeared to be one of the brightest talents to come through the English academy system. And in the summer of 2008, at the age of 16, he joined Tottenham for £700,000 from Crystal Palace. However since his move to Spurs the career of Bostock has been in decline. The reason, many say, is that that he moved too early and that he should have continued with his development at Crystal Palace. After signing Bostock, Spurs sent him out on loan and since 2008 Bostock has played for Brentford, Hull City, Sheffield Wednesday, Swindon Town and now for Toronto in the MLS. He has barely played regularly for any of these clubs. It must be hard for him to be moving to new clubs and new environments constantly. Where is the stability? He is still only 21 yet the key development years between 16 and 21 have been effectively ruined because of his move to Spurs.

Those who think he moved 'too early' may be right when we see other players progress and develop at the club before making the step up - players like Wilfried Zaha, Nathaniel Clyne and Victor Moses who have all become top players in the past few years.

By staying at Palace these youngsters have played in a side which they know, close to their families, and in a comfortable environment. If they had left early, like Bostock, would they have been in the same situation as him now? The Bostock story highlights the ills of moving to a new club between 15 and 18, where opportunity to play and progress is minimal.

A similar story can be seen with two young Leeds players. In 2006 Chelsea bought Leeds academy players Tom Taiwo and Michael Woods for a total of £5m when they were both 16 years old. However, just like Bostock, both players found opportunities limited and they quite simply stopped progressing.

As Taiwo said in an interview with the *Daily Mail*, in October 2011, "At 16 I was rated as a very good prospect; now I'm at Carlisle. You see boys who weren't rated at 16 who at 23 are playing for England. Chris Smalling, he was playing non-League. Now he's a top player with Manchester United and England. It makes a mockery of the academy system, shows it is not the be-all and end-all. Boys like myself have been right through the system and now I'm nowhere near his standard. That's the worry."

Both Taiwo and Woods are now playing for Hibernian and Harrogate, which would highlight a serious problem of moving to one of the 'rich' clubs. A lack of opportunity, the pressure to justify a big price tag and a failure to understand that these young lads are still developing and still require support. Chelsea in particular appears to be an 'academy' which leads to career suicide.

> The top clubs don't learn, they are obsessed with getting players at a young age and appear unwilling to develop them or give them the opportunity to improve. It would be best for these clubs to allow these players to stay with the clubs they are developing at.

# Buying up the best talent, yet any first team action?

Problems can also be seen at Manchester City. Vast wealth and unlimited resources have allowed them to go around Europe and pick up the brightest talent around. Nationality has become irrelevant and, as their first team shows, being English is not relevant. City has been scouring the world for young talent as they seek to build a squad for the future.

Karim Rekik signed for Manchester City from Feyenoord in the summer of 2011 and set a club record when he turned out for the last 12 minutes of the Carling Cup win over Birmingham, aged 16 years 294 days. Marcos Lopes, a Brazilian born attacking midfielder cost the Blues around £790,000. Lopes is a Portugal Under-16 and Under-17 international and was snapped up from the Benfica youth ranks as a 15-year-old. Jules Olivier Ntcham is regarded as one of the most promising youngsters in France and was the captain of France's Under-16 squad.

Perhaps the two biggest signings that City have made have been the Spanish players Denis Suárez and Jose Angel Pozo. Suárez signed for the club on 23 May 2011 and City beat off interest from Barcelona, Chelsea and rivals Manchester United signing him from Celta Vigo for an initial fee of £850,000 that could rise by £2.75 million depending on appearances and performances. And in Pozo, Manchester City showed their financial clout by paying Real Madrid £3.5m for the 15-year-old starlet. The deal could eventually be worth £5million.

Yet can you see City really integrating young academy players into the first team? Even Suárez has struggled to break through. Perhaps the case of John Guidetti highlights the problems with big teams integrating young players. In April 2008, at the age of sixteen, he signed a three-year deal with City. Although he showed his quality in the youth ranks, he was not given a chance in the first team. A loan move to Feyenoord in 2011/12 proved his talents where he scored 20 goals in 23 games for the Dutch club. Many City fans have shown a desire to have him become a part of City's senior team. Yet there is not a chance he will be given a go at City. As Twente chairman Joop Munsterman said regarding Guidetti "The most important thing for a young player like Guidetti is that he plays a lot of games."

Nick Powell, now at Manchester United, is a perfect example of why staying at a lower league team can be the best option. Powell joined Crewe as young lad and at 16 made his debut for the first team in August 2010 - becoming the second youngest player to play for Crewe. Between 2010 and 2012 he was given the opportunity to play and develop and, in total, played 55 games for the club.

His performances in 2011/12, in particular, alerted many to his potential, enough so that United bought him for £4m in the summer of 2012. Imagine if Powell had left Crewe at 16, would he have been given the opportunity to play and develop like he did at Crewe? Not a chance. The hope now is that he is given the opportunities at Old Trafford to help progress his career further.

# Dario Gradi's project

The story of Nick Powell allows us to look at Crewe Alexandra and discuss one of the top developers of talent in the country. Crewe is perhaps one of the best examples of a club who are doing it right in terms of youth development. They use their academy for what it should be for: to develop players for the first team. Their success is down to one man, Dario Gradi.

Gradi's philosophy is simple yet effective. In an interview with *The Guardian* he explained that "With kids we talk about can you get hold of the ball and can you do something with it. Can you keep the ball? Can you pass and move?" Simple, and you can see why Crewe has developed good footballers like Nick Powell, and Ashley Westwood who moved to Aston Villa in 2012 and who has developed into an excellent player. Before them players like Danny Murphy, David Platt, and Dean Ashton also came through the Crewe system. The work Gradi has done is respected and valued across the game.

Yet this has led to the problem discussed above: the 'poaching' of talent. The issue for Crewe is that the bigger clubs start to come looking for their players even earlier. As Gradi says, "We have a situation where one of our 15-year-olds has been approached. He is an outstanding player by any standards and he has come in and told us that he wants to leave right now to join a big club."

"We lost a 12-year-old to Everton. He was our best 12-year-old. The lure is that the bigger clubs pay big expenses. This kid will be getting several hundred pounds a week in expenses. We pay expenses but nothing like that. It's more a case of giving out £20 if someone can pick a kid up en route. It is so hard to protect your players. All this goes against the morality of the game – it's the rich robbing the poor," explained Gradi.

> The big clubs are poaching other club's players. One should worry, financially, for the smaller clubs who lose out on a player's true, long-term, value.

As we saw in Chapter Six, under the new EPPP rules, Category One clubs are free to take the best players from lower category clubs with minimal compensation. Should they really be able to 'poach' the best talent from clubs around them if they have no inclination to actually give players the opportunity for first team football?

Crewe Alexandra accept they will lose players to bigger clubs, yet they proved what they are doing is working when on the 30th April 2013, Steve Davis, the Crewe Manager, gave Gradi his dream of having an all academy starting XI. It was an affirmation for all the work and dedication to youth development that Gradi and

Crewe had put in - from a manager who believes in giving youth a chance. And they won 2-0.

The issue of smaller clubs losing their best players is obviously a worry for England's future. If the top clubs want to buy these young players and actually play them and give them experience of top level football both domestically and in Europe then there is no problem. Yet if they wish to simply 'hoard' them in their youth sides and restrict their development then what value is there? Especially when sides like Crewe and Crystal Palace have actually shown a willingness to develop players to play senior football, and not just use their academy as a showpiece to make the club look good.

# Agent issues

It would be foolish and naïve to address the issues of youth development without discussing football agents where, unfortunately, the interests of the player (football wise) are often neglected in favour of financial gain.

Let us look at Chelsea once again. Ruben Loftus-Cheek has been at Chelsea's academy since he was an Under-8. Now 17 years old the midfielder has become a very bright prospect indeed; he is still to play a competitive senior game for the first team. On his 17th birthday he signed a new contract which over two-and-half years would see him make over a £1 million. His agent, Joseph Donkor, also made £1 million from the deal for 'arranging' the contract.

The issue of high wages for young players as well as agents 'meddling' with these players has led to outrage from many. When David Pleat heard about the contract - he was amazed; speaking in the *Daily Mirror* Pleat proclaimed that, "The whole thing is crazy. The scramble for the best schoolboys, fuelled by agents, leads to wholly inflated earning figures. It gives the youngsters a false sense of perspective – both about football and about life. It is madness. I remember when there used to be a cap on what you earned until you played your first professional game. Nowadays a kid won't sign on as an apprentice for a club until he is guaranteed 'x' amount of money. There should be a limit on what clubs offer."

Pleat is absolutely correct. These players are becoming rich before they even make the senior side, they are not being treated like players who need 'development' but as players who are 'already there'. Yet they have done nothing to earn these wages except play for a club where the value of money means little. What will happen to players like Ruben Loftus-Cheek? Well, what usually happens to teenage millionaires? A loss of focus and a lack of determination to improve because the club have effectively taken away his motivation.

> Because of the vast wealth in the English game players
> are being treated as commodities in order for
> agents to make big money.

Go to a club lower down the pecking order though and you see wages which reflect the league and age of the player. What will these players do? Work harder to improve. Unfortunately clubs like Chelsea and Manchester City are devaluing work rate by paying players wages they don't deserve or need and then pricing them out of the market for clubs who could actually use them and develop them further. It is madness.

## Lessons from Germany

The correlation between more money and fewer players coming through the academies is worrying for English football. In Germany, sides like Dortmund have been forced into using their academy players because of financial difficulties but they are now regarded as one of Europe's best sides. Their story really is fantastic - it is all about high quality youth development and, importantly, giving players between16 and 21 a chance to develop. Out of necessity perhaps, but successful nonetheless.

> German football as a whole has benefited from an
> investment in youth development and we are now seeing a
> prosperous league and national team.

Perhaps the most important part of Germany's resurgence has been their adoption of the 6+5 rule which FIFA put forward. In 2003/04 Germany had 44% foreign players playing in the Bundesliga, and they realised something needed to change. Today it is 38%, which means the Bundesliga has 62% of their players, playing each week, who are able to play for the national team. In England the numbers are reversed.

As we have seen, the 'home grown' rule in England is ambiguous and clubs have abused it. In Germany they develop more 'home grown' players because their rules state that at least 12 players in each academy's intake have to be eligible to play for Germany. Simply put the German model gives more domestic players the chance play more, meaning more players gain the necessary experience to improve.

The top clubs and Premier League are doing a disservice to the English game by not creating more opportunities for clubs to develop talent. If every academy had the same rule as Germany's academies then the quality would surely improve. The Premier League, if they genuinely did care about the development of the national side, would make academy teams use the 6+5 rule, or would make the 'home grown' rule less ambiguous. At this moment it is clear that they have no interest in England's national side. The Premier League needs to do more to prove they care.

# Bridging the gap

Between 17 and 21 years of age, players need more guidance and help than before; they are mixing with adults and playing at the senior levels, while still learning about themselves and developing as young men. This is a major period in their lives, and careers, and there is not enough being done to bridge the gap between youth and senior football. Expectations are placed too high, at an early age, on too many young shoulders, which increases the pressure and makes the task of improving harder.

Clubs need to bridge the gap between youth and senior football much more effectively and as sides like Chelsea and Manchester City are showing, for all the money spent on facilities, coaching, and wages, if they cannot integrate these young players into the first team squad then what really is the point?

Josh McEachran is a prime example. A player with such potential at 16 has not progressed for four years due to a lack of experience and stability. Compare McEachran to players like Jack Wilshere and Tom Cleverly whose loan careers at Bolton and Wigan were successful in terms of playing time and working with coaches who play football in an attacking, technical style. There is no doubt that these players benefited from these experiences as loan deals are not 'bad' in themselves, with experience and playing time fundamental to improvement. However loan deals need to make sense in terms of style and environment.

This is why the 'B' team idea has been put forward by certain people. If we take Barcelona as a model then it is clear why they are able to produce players who play the 'Barca' way. Through having a 'B' side that plays in the professional league they are able to give players valuable competitive experience while playing the same style and method as the first team. Their success with player development comes from consistency. From the youth levels to the senior side - all teams play the same way in terms of tactics and style. All the players therefore know the system inside out by the time they reach the first team.

The introduction of 'B' teams in England may have a positive impact on developing more cohesion and continuity between the youth and senior set-ups. However, it's an unlikely development to come. Greater hope and trust must be put on the EPPP's Under-21 league.

The new EPPP Under-21 league is supposed to be the bridge between the youth and first team and there is clearly a benefit and need for this type of league. The removal of the reserve league (in place of the Under-21 league) points towards a change of mentality from a place to 'hoard' senior players who are not part of first team plans, or who are coming back from injury, to one where the team and players are viewed as individuals being developed.

Rafa Benitez believes the Under-21 league could help to develop players in England. He says that, "From my personal experience as a player and coach in Spain for more than 30 years I would say that two basic things would help: first, youth system coaches' formation; second, the Under-21 competition system."

Hopefully the Under-21 league will bring the desired effect yet perhaps players should still seek a move to sides in the Championship in order to further their development and receive playing opportunities. Tom Ince is a great example of a player who moved to the Championship and whose career has excelled and blossomed because of it. His time at Liverpool surely gave him a good foundation yet playing continually at Blackpool between the ages of 19 and 21 (he has played over 85 games for Blackpool) has certainly aided and accelerated his development. Would he have got this experience at Liverpool? Not to this level. At Chelsea or Manchester City? Never.

Moving 'down' actually made Tom Ince a better player.

> Academies need to provide their players with experience, opportunity and continuity all the way through their developmental years.

# Summary

The problem with sides like Manchester City and Chelsea, and others across Europe like Madrid and PSG, is that they are clubs with the means to buy in the best talent and thus don't *need* youth academies. The irony is that they are very good developers of young players because they can afford the best facilities and coaching. However if they cannot offer these players a route to the professional game between 17 and 21 then they are doing a disservice to their players.

If we don't give our young players, both domestic and foreign, the chance to develop fully up to the age of 21, then we run the risk of seriously harming their careers. The truth is that too many big clubs appear to treat players selfishly by hoarding them in their academies without the intention to push them onto the next level. It would be better for these clubs to allow these players to leave and let them sign for sides who will give them the valuable opportunities needed to take their game to the next level. English football cannot have more Josh McEachrans or John Bostocks, whose careers are wasted by the big clubs.

For clubs like Crewe and Southampton youth development is not a 'bit of fun', like Chelsea and Manchester City appear to treat it. For them youth development is a key and fundamental aspect to securing the long term future of their clubs. For the good of England's football future this is how youth development should be treated.

# Part III

# Finding The Talent

# 15
# The Importance of Opportunity

*"We overlook just how large a role we all play and by 'we' I mean society, in determining who makes it and who doesn't."* Malcolm Gladwell.

## The fortunate few

Up until now we have discussed extensively the development of young footballers, notably their quest to hit 10,000 hours, as well as the importance of coaching and the environment they learn in. These areas have been shown to be key for the development of elite players. In this part of the book we will look into the importance of other fundamental factors which start a young player on their journey to the professional game. We will start with 'opportunity'.

In his book, *Outliers*, Malcolm Gladwell explains that people simply do not rise from nothing and that each individual is not afforded the same opportunities. Gladwell argues that, "parenting and patronage are important" and that those who rise to the top are, "often the beneficiaries of hidden advantages and extraordinary opportunity." In turn, Matthew Syed, the author of *Bounce*, demolishes the idea that talent is the key to success. He tackles the myth of 'natural-born' talent and confirms what we have discussed already: that it is practice rather than talent that creates elite performance. For Syed, the top athletes have completed more hours of 'deliberate' practice than their lower skilled peers. He argues that child prodigies, such as Mozart and Tiger Woods, actually back up this theory. They just started intensive practice much earlier than everyone else and were thus more advanced than their peers, which of course made them look more 'natural'.

Syed uses himself as an example to illustrate how his career path developed because of the opportunity he was afforded as young child. His career as an Olympic table tennis player came about because the head sports coach at Syed's primary school was a table tennis fanatic. Syed and his classmates were invited to join the local table tennis club and from there they developed and mastered their table tennis skills.

The importance of this opportunity cannot be overstated. For a period in the 1980s, Syed's neighbourhood produced a disproportionate number of the UK's outstanding table tennis players; amazingly six of them lived on Syed's street.

> Although genetics play a part, it is opportunity which defines a person's path and destiny.

Syed makes the point that if he had lived one road down from where he did, he would have gone to a different school, where he would never have met the teacher who inspired him and who gave him invaluable hours of practice. Living on a different street would have meant completely different opportunities and a different future path. Most likely his table tennis career would never have happened. His opportunity came about by luck and - through that - he worked hard, developed his skills, and became an elite table tennis player.

Syed believes that a "combination of opportunity (being in the right place at the right time) and hard work," are essential for success. If we consider football, then a young player's progression may be, in large part, based on an individual's opportunity to find the right school, the right teacher, or coach. It may have to do with having parents who love or played sport, or something as simple as access to a car so they can drive their child, and support their opportunities.

The message which underpins the modern thinking of elite development is that innate talent is not as important as opportunity, because opportunity gives a young performer the chance to develop and master their abilities and thus hone and refine their skills. It enables them to clock up more hours on the quest for that golden 10,000. These chances make a difference and, as Syed's story illustrates, it really does matter when and where you grew up.

Carol Dweck, author of *Mindset*, makes clear that people have different resources and opportunities; for example – "people with money have a safety net, so they can take more risks, they can keep going longer until they succeed." She adds, "People with easy access to a good education, people with a network of influential friends, and people who know to be in the right place at the right time all stand a better chance of having their efforts pay off."

> The pathway to becoming an elite footballer is based on the environment and opportunity afforded.

# The importance of when you're born

Perhaps the most fortunate opportunity a young footballer may enjoy is their month of birth. Birth effect is something which is very difficult to manage yet very easy to understand. In England the school year goes from September 1st – August 31st the following year. It is thus conceivable that in a game of football there may be two players who are separated by 364 days, effectively a year apart. A boy who turns ten on September 1$^{st}$ could be playing against another boy who won't turn ten until August 31$^{st}$ the following year. And as Gladwell points out, "a twelve month gap represents an enormous difference in physical maturity."

Now this is a major issue in the development of elite athletes; although puberty and maturation occur at different times for each person, the majority of players born earlier will develop earlier and will thus be stronger, taller and perhaps quicker too. Also they will more than likely be a 'better' player because they may have simply practiced more. They appear a better player to many and are thus regarded as *talented*. This is the flaw of football academies and youth sports all over the world.

> The issue of 'relative age effect' is starting to be appreciated as the single most important facet of elite development.

A study in the *Journal of Sports Sciences* carried out by Helsen *et al.* (2005) confirmed the story behind relative age effect. They found that talent selection procedures employed in many sports tend to discriminate in favour of players who are born early in the selection year, typically those who are physically stronger and who also profit from other advantages associated with the relative age effect (e.g. more experience) rather than those who are born later in the selection year. The researchers found a clear relative age effect for all the national youth selections in the Under-15, Under-16, Under-17 and Under-18 age categories

In a separate study, by Vaeyens *et al.* (2008), researchers found a growing agreement that traditional cross-sectional talent identification models are likely to exclude many, especially late maturing, 'promising' children from development programmes due to the dynamic and multidimensional nature of sport talent. Furthermore, Ben Oakley from the Open University has highlighted that, in 2009, "professional English youth academies (aged 16-20 years) were grossly over-represented by players with birthdates in a three month period." It was found that, "57% of youngsters were born in September, November or December whilst only 14% celebrated their birthday in June, July or August."

It is therefore conceivable that there are players with real talent and skill who have been disregarded because they are being judged against players who are almost a year older. Realistically, players born in May, June, July and August are most often denied valuable opportunities - all because of the month they were born.

> It is clear that when you were born has a big impact on your chances of sporting success.

## The age bias advantage

*"The simple fact is that adults have voted them out of the game because of our desire to pick bigger, stronger, faster players."* Nick Levett.

Mike Duncan, a sport science lecturer at Coventry University, argues that relative age effect arose from, "the consequences of grouping young boys for entry into organized sport, thereby producing a one-year age range for participants." He points out that, "As size, speed, and coordination are highly correlated with age, older players within the age-group will, on average, show superior performance. This has resulted in maturity being mistaken for ability." Those who are bigger at a young age are perceived as more skilful and talented and are then afforded those early advantages and opportunities which Gladwell discusses.

And what happens when bigger, stronger, faster players are 'chosen'? As Gladwell writes, "He is selected and gets better coaching, his teammates get better, he plays more games against better opponents at better facilities; effectively he experiences more 'deliberate' practice."

As he then points out, "At the start, this advantage isn't so much that he is better but that he is older, yet by the age of thirteen or fourteen with the benefit of better coaching and all that extra practice he really is better. Now he is more likely to make it." And it all comes from the fact he was born in September.

Compare this to the player who was born late in the year; he misses out on expert coaching, great facilities, and a higher level of competition and ultimately is denied the opportunity to become elite.

Duncan believes that relative age effect is, "strikingly evident in activities that are competitive and where performance is highly correlated with age and maturity." Coaches and academies appear to take the heaviest and or tallest because it is often the 'easiest' option.

The problem with youth sports, according to Ben Oakley, is that adults often believe size and coordination advantages translate into better performances. Football and ice hockey coaches faced with selecting their teams often confuse talent with age and, often unknowingly, select a team with larger youngsters that are more likely to win.

> Can it be true that we simply associate better
> performance with being older?

An indication of the bias which relative age effect produces was seen at the FIFA Under-17 World Cup in 2005 where the winners Mexico had 95% (19/20) of their squad born in the first six months of their yearly cut off. No players were present who were born in the last three months. Similarly, Brazil had 70% in the first 6 months and just one player who was born in the last 3 months. This is not a one off.

At a recent Under-17 European Championship, 75% of the footballers were born in a four month window. Europe differs to England in terms of their age-banding which is why many of their players are born between January and April. Andy Roxburgh, UEFA's technical director, told *The Observer*, "Approximately 75% of the players (in the Under-17 European championship) were in the January to April category. To put it another way, if you're born on the 26 or 27 of December you've got a problem getting selected for national youth teams."

The new EPPP plans seek to put the best with best and thus develop higher quality players, yet nowhere is there any solution (or ideas) on how to tackle birth effect. The worry is that a boy born August 31st may never get an opportunity, yet with the right 'opportunities' he may have been something special. Imagine if he had been born just a day later. That is how essential opportunity can be in determining a future elite player.

> It is evident that players born earlier in the year benefit
> from a judgement bias which puts more value
> on height and mass in the performance assessment.

## Self-esteem issues

In addition to differences in physical maturation from the relative age effect, those born early in the year may also be more psychologically mature than their counterparts. A 'chosen' player may feel more confident, they have been 'selected' and this success can increase motivation and encourage older players to continue practising in an attempt to achieve further success. The opposite process can arise for those born later in the year, potentially reducing their motivation to continue to participate in any given sport.

As Helsen *et al.* (2005) argue in their study, on relative age effect across youth academies in football, "The self-image and self-esteem of any child will be affected favourably by success and unfavourably by failure if the cause is perceived to be internally mediated." By this they mean that children's perceptions of success or failure are often attributed towards themselves. Those young children who are born later in the cut-off year are therefore more likely to miss out when it comes to being selected and may attribute that 'failure' to themselves. Helsen and colleagues believe that this may impact upon children's levels of self-esteem and potential to "drop out" of sport.

## Solutions to relative age effect

Several solutions to the relative age effect have been proposed in the literature. But first let us consider what Belgium's FA has done to tackle relative age effect.

Belgium is once again ahead of England in terms of youth development and relative age effects. They understand that players who mature early have a physical advantage when compared to their later maturing peers. They know that differences in players between 10 and 16 can be very defined and that there is an unequal battle between early and late maturing players.

So what does Belgium do? The FA publishes a rather impressive magazine, called *The Bootroom,* and in one recent article they conducted interviews with different coaches across Belgium's youth development setup. In fascinating depth and clarity it appears that Belgium's approach to talent identification is what is aiding their recent success in developing top professionals.

First off, they identify players at Under-14 level, which is in stark contrast to England where players are being scouted and judged from as young as 6 or 7 years old. The Head of the Belgian FA's national teams, Marc Van Geersom, makes the case that "It's so difficult to say who is talented. Sometimes the later you start the better it is."

The Belgian approach takes maturation effects into account and thus allows a larger pool of players to be developed. Late development is a big issue for Van Geersom and one he wishes to overcome, "I'm always talking about our late developers. It's a project we've had for years now."

To enhance the opportunity of late developers Belgium's academies have two sides from Under-14 upwards. One of these two sides caters specifically for the late developers (either physical or mental lateness) enabling them to receive the high quality coaching and hours that those who mature early benefit from and which is necessary for elite development. Belgium's approach has led to an enviable talent pipeline. England could learn from Belgium's development model where they cater for late developers and those who, in England, might be deemed 'too small'.

Is England suffering because we are judging players too early? Are we not taking maturation effects into account, and are thus preventing players from staying 'in the system'? Are our late developers being deprived of the valuable practice which is necessary to reach elite levels? In all cases it appears the answer is yes.

Other solutions have been proposed for combating the relative age effect issue. Firstly, it has been suggested that a two year banding or even three year banding will potentially cover variations in maturation effects. Those players born between May and August may have more opportunity this way. Yet this situation is not simple, if you split the year into two bands, the same situation (where each band gets front loaded) could arise. And changing the bandings, as per Spain, from January 1st to December 31st brings familiar problems; for Spain, more players are distributed in the January to April part of the year.

Perhaps allowing more movement up and down age groups, based on biological age (or relative age within a year), is a step forward. Another suggestion is a yearly rotation and cut-off dates which would mean all players would experience the advantage of a higher relative age group at some point in their football career. This idea, that youth football should promote more movement between age bandings, is an interesting one. The late developers may benefit from playing in a lower age group in order to help them enjoy their football. Conversely, stronger and more mature players will benefit from playing up a level.

Another solution is simply to focus on aspects of football which can benefit the 'late developers' or the smaller players. The creation of development centres across the country which focus more on skill and tactical development over strength will benefit more players and increase the talent pool. Through this, smaller players can develop their skills and the confidence to progress further.

Naturally, a key solution is to change the mentality of youth team coaches. This comes back to the 'win at all costs' culture, of course. Coaches should be encouraged to change their philosophical prejudices. In fairness, the new FA youth modules do focus more education on maturation and relative age effects which should improve coaches' knowledge and help them approach late developers better.

> The hope is that coaches will pay more attention to
> developing the technical and tactical skills of players instead
> of over-relying on physical characteristics such as height.

## Summary

In England, we need to change how we view youth players. We can learn from other countries that it is not size which matters, but what the player is capable of, over the longer term!

As the next chapter will discuss, it is the scouts and academies which need to radically overhaul their talent identification methods to improve the quality and quantity of players coming through the academy system.

# 16

# Talent Identification

*"If you don't get the recruitment right the rest is a waste of time."* Brian Jones.

We just saw the importance of opportunity and a player's birth date and how these two things could have a major impact on the future of a young player. It is therefore essential to assess the people (and methods) that form the bridge between the foundation levels and academy football - the 'scouts'.

The key to finding the best talent comes from those men who travel around local parks on the weekends aiming to find the most talented players. The pro-academies have a large network of scouts who watch games and tournaments all over the country. The aim of these clubs is to identify the best individuals for their academies; to try to find players who have the potential to become a professional footballer. However, as this chapter will discuss, it is the 'recruitment' aspect which is preventing England from developing a higher number of quality players.

## Experts or amateurs?

*"In the majority of cases the key to a child's footballing future has been turned by wild hunches, guesswork, and dare I say it, decisions made sometimes on the way a child may 'look'. Is this good enough?"* Peter Glynn, FA Skills coach.

Talent identification programmes usually examine and judge a player from watching them compete in a match, then assessing their performance. If the player is deemed 'good enough' they are invited to an academy for a six week 'trial'. It is here where the players are judged against the level of the academy boys. Now it is not easy to identify all the small attributes and details that join together to make someone capable of becoming a professional footballer at the highest level. It takes an analytical and focused mind, with a disciplined personality, to watch the game as a professional scout.

Vaeyens *et al.* (2008) point out that the success rates of talent identification and development programmes have rarely been assessed and the validity of the models applied remains highly debated. They argue that talent identification and development programmes should be dynamic and interconnected taking into consideration 'maturity status' and the potential to develop rather than the exclusion of children at an early age.

So if talent identification needs to be improved in England what should we be looking for?

## Judging too early

We have spoken already about the issues of early specialisation and how it may actually be detrimental for talented players to go into 'full time' football coaching at an early age. Yet the battle to sign the best players has intensified into little more than an undignified scramble with clubs increasingly searching for younger and younger players. Academies fear that they will miss out to rival clubs and thus aim to sign players as young as possible. It has led to a scattergun approach to scouting.

> Based on the type of players who are 'recruited' by scouts, it is evident that their approach is myopic and basic.

Can we seriously judge the potential of a player as a 9, 10 or *even* 11-year-old? Is it not just too early? Would it not be better if young players were allowed to progress at the grassroots level, to enjoy their sport at a young age - being able to take part in a wider variety of sports which has been seen to aid their development?

As witnessed in Chapter Ten there is a strong argument to be made for young children taking part in a multitude of sports - to enrich their multi-functional development. At 11+ players will possess more functionality, agility and speed than their specialised counterparts. And this is being seen in academies. At Under-12 and Under-14 levels, scouts are having to go in search of fresh players to make up for those already in the system who appear to lack good movement and speed. The fact they have been at the club since eight should be an indicator of the failing here.

Perhaps the best example of a 'late' addition to the academy system is Theo Walcott. Andy Ritchie, a youth coach at Southampton said that he hadn't seen anything like him before. Walcott was 13 when he first experienced academy football; he scored a hat trick for Southampton in his first game versus Chelsea. From there it was a meteoric rise to professional football.

Yet perhaps the fact he came to academy football late was the reason he looked so 'natural'. He only started playing football at 10 years old. As Walcott professes, "As a little kid, I wasn't even interested in football." What this example highlights is the potential benefit of players developing their all-round sporting prowess. Being recruited early and playing academy football at a young age prevents this.

> By scouting players too early - are scouts and academies negatively affecting young players' development?

# The English academy premium

*"At the club level [you must] have open-mindedness. You used to get all this stuff from the scouts, don't bring me back a centre-half unless he's 6ft 1in. That means [Carlos] Puyol [the captain] wouldn't get a game for Barcelona."* Andy Roxburgh.

As well as scouting players at a young age, perhaps academies need to re-evaluate their approach and how they actually assess players. What are they looking for? This is a question which is starting to be asked more and more by coaches in the grassroots and academy game.

We have already discussed why certain players will be more physically developed than others (mainly due to their age in the school year) yet, to the chagrin of many coaches, too many scouts demonstrate little knowledge about this. Scouts' failure to understand or appreciate relative age effect is a major issue and it is not being given enough attention.

As Tom Taiwo said in his interview with the *Daily Mail* "Not enough account is being taken of boys' 'peaks and troughs', of differing rates of physical and emotional development."

Now there are various factors which are important to understand and evaluate when identifying talent.

- Physical Factors

- Physiological Factors

- Sociological Factors

- Psychological Factors

Dr Mike Duncan, of Coventry University, believes that "Despite on-going attempts, science and practice has still not found a means to accurately identify talented individuals whether it be in a specific sport or another domain." Yet when you see players who are brought in to academies on trial they most often possess the defining features of relative age effect: they are bigger, stronger and faster than many their age. Is it conceivable that scouts are simply recruiting the most 'developed' players - believing that they are more talented than their counterparts, some of whom (as we saw in the previous chapter) are almost a year younger? It appears so.

> It seems that many scouts have been given the remit to find the biggest and strongest players on the pitch.

Let me give you an example. A young player of nine years old arrived at a local professional academy and impressed the coaches who worked with him. When one approached the assistant head scout they asked his opinion. His answer was worrying for England's future; "His Dad's not big enough," was his response. Size really should not have any bearing on the player, especially one who played in an attacking role.

Yet perhaps the worst part of this story was that the player's father was actually a professional footballer who had enjoyed an illustrious career in the Premier League and who had scored hundreds of goals during his time there. His size had not prevented him from becoming a top professional yet, according to this scout, his son would be judged on what his father looked like, more than what the young lad was capable of himself.

The 'what if' scenario is always interesting when we consider English coaching and recruitment. Imagine what some of the greats of football were like when they were younger and how the English 'mentality' would have affected their potential careers. Would Cruyff, Best, or Messi have made it out of the English system? Probably not. And why is this? Because England are looking for the wrong thing when they scout for 'potential'. Let us see why Holland and Barcelona's philosophies towards talent identification make their production systems so fruitful.

Holland is a small country with a small population yet is a giant in the game. The Dutch model of player development is arguably the best model of player development in the world. In his book, *Beautiful Orange*, David Winner talks of Dutch football being admired in all parts of the world and how their style requires high individual skill and intelligent combined team play. They have produced great players who possess creative skill and intelligence.

Players like Johann Cruyff, Dennis Bergkamp and Wesley Sneijder have all come through Ajax's famed academy, so what do Ajax look for when scouting young players? They base their assessments of players on four aspects. They call it the TIPS code, an acronym for Technique, Intelligence, Personality and Speed.

Through the TIPS model of selection, the scouts and coaches at Ajax take the following into account when scouting and identifying talent: a player's relationship with the ball, his temperament in competition, his intelligence, movement, understanding, his ability to learn, take on information and his attitude, listening skills, and his willingness to learn. Looking at this list makes you realise why Holland is constantly developing talented players.

Barcelona, who adopted the Ajax model of youth development several decades ago with the arrival of Rinus Michels and then Johann Cruyff, use the talent identification of TABS: Technique, Attitude, Balance and Speed.

The Barcelona and Ajax academies can be said to be the most productive and successful in world football, constantly producing players for the professional game. The adage of 'what you put in is what you get out' is precisely what talent identification and academies are proving. Ajax and Barcelona are scouting a particular type of player and reaping the rewards of it.

# England's failure to produce small players

Size isn't everything in football. Players like Pele and Maradona were no giants, and over the past decade we have witnessed the rise of the 'little man' in football. With the success of Barcelona and players like Xavi, Iniesta and Lionel Messi – it can be shown that you don't have to be tall to be successful. In fact these players have proven that being small is advantageous.

Over the past several seasons we have started to see a change in English football with the arrival of many smaller players. The lessons learnt from Barcelona and Spain with their quality of football and success has brought to England players like Carlos Tevez, Sergio Aguero, Eden Hazard, German player of the year Shinji

Kagawa, and Spanish players Cesc Fabregas, Santi Cazorla, Juan Mata and David Silva.

> The clichéd 'not big enough' mantra coming from academies and scouts is restricting the development of our own Xavis and Messis.

This is a positive sign that the English style and tactics are modernising and that the quality and type of player being sought is different to that of previous decades. Evidently English clubs, or at least their foreign coaches, have seen the importance of possessing the modern *trequarista*: the small, creative playmaker who enhances their attacking quality and creativity.

Ten years ago, you'd have said football was becoming a game for physical monsters, but the success of the little man has alerted many to the potential of these players. So why are these smaller players seemingly better in these positions? Well it has to do with the restricted space and time in the modern game. This has meant that players need to be excellent at finding and exploiting space as well as possessing first-class technical ability, poise and vision. The smaller player has proven to have these characteristics in abundance and have become essential for sides looking to bridge the gap between midfield and attack to unlock tight defences. Playmakers have become the most important players on the pitch and the 'little man' is proving to be the most capable in that role.

As the world of football has embraced the smaller players, only two 'little men' have been effective for English football in recent years and in both cases have been under-used or not used effectively for their national side. Paul Scholes and Joe Cole could have been very special players for England and yet were not deemed as important as Gerrard or Lampard in the 'playmaker' role. Both ended up being shunted to the left side of the team. England's mentality towards 'small' players has proven damaging in the past decade yet perhaps the most concerning part is how small players are viewed in England's youth academies.

England's problem appears to be a mistrust of 'small' players. Without question the single most important change - which needs to happen in the majority of English clubs - is for them to dismiss the notion that 'small' players are less valuable than bigger players.

Arsenal appears to be one of the only English teams who favour technical ability over size. Wenger's project has been in place at Arsenal for 15 years and working with Liam Brady, the academy manager, young players are being developed in a similar style to Barcelona's. Changes in youth development often take a decade to see and this is the case at Arsenal. Jack Wilshere is the first world class product to come through the club's academy, a true mark of what they can produce. Other academies need to understand the value this 'type' of player brings to a side and not dismiss them based solely on their height.

> If England wishes to compete with the top sides then our attack needs more creative 'little men' playing, which will allow England to be more creative in possession.

# Summary

The gap between grassroots football and academy football is bridged by some of the most important people in the development of elite athletes - scouts. It is therefore shocking and nonsensical to have people with little or no understanding of the game, and children, to be scouting games and finding players. In England, 'scouts' are, for the most part, amateurs who have little knowledge of talent identification.

As this chapter highlights, English scouts are failing to see what is required in the modern game and are basing their opinions on players who possess size and strength over other more valuable capacities.

English football needs to change its approach to identifying talent and instead look towards characteristics of the modern game. Ajax have proven that their model of talent identification locates the talented players not for the short term but for the future. English scouting has a long way to go. And as the next chapter will discuss physical aspects should not be seen as important a focus. Scouts should be looking at what a player possesses 'between the ears'.

# 17

# The Best Indicator of Success

*"Those who make it need to be intelligent."* Johan Cruyff.

## The failings of brawn over brains

Physical attributes are a major part of football: speed, strength, spring and stamina are all essential components of the game, yet what is also important are the mental skills of intelligence, anticipation, composure, decision making and positioning. I don't believe we look for these faculties in young players, nor do we coach it enough.

When you watch many English players do you see readers of the game, or reactors to the game? There is a common flaw within English development that we develop players who are reactive, who rely more on the voice of the coach than their own brain. Reading the game is an essential part of modern day football. There is little room for 'reactive' players as the game is so quick, where a moment's hesitation or loss of concentration is punished.

In the previous chapter we looked at the premium which English scouts put on physicality, yet it appears evident that scouts should be looking for players with skills of anticipation and concentration. It is a player's intelligence and *willingness to learn* which should be central to any scout's judgement. Scouts should be looking for 'smart' footballers.

# Seeking out intelligence

Football intelligence is about the work a player does both in and out of possession. When in possession the best players are able to see the game and make quick and successful judgements on the best options available. Decision making is a key component of football intelligence. Off the ball the best players are able to find and exploit space in order to penetrate the opposition. Awareness of the opposition, teammates and space is a key component for effective football performance.

Let us return again to Belgium and their impressive achievements when developing youth. For a country and league like Belgium's - it is almost a necessity to develop youngsters. With no money comes a greater reliance on developing your own talent and perhaps this is why they have achieved such success in recent years. We saw their approach to late developers previously, yet perhaps the most significant part of their talent identification model is that they seek out youth players who possess intelligence and decision making strengths. They want to find players who can read the game.

The Belgian FA put together six factors which they believe a top player requires. They are as follows:

- A winner's mentality
- Emotional stability
- Personality
- Explosiveness
- Insight in the game
- Ball and body control

Scouts in Belgium are instructed to use this as their framework for identifying talent. A player's intelligence is thought to be the difference between an average and good individual. In turn, the Belgian FA seeks to educate coaches to 'see' the players who understand the game. When they find those with intelligence, they move them into the appropriate schools and development programs in order to give them the quality coaching required to take them to the top of the game.

> Belgium's success in youth development has come from their scouting of players possessing intelligence.

# Does skill matter?

There are those who believe that the best indicator of a player's talent is their skill level. Wilson *et al.* (2010), for example, have suggested that motor skill performance specific to football is the most important indicator of football performance. Tottenham Hotspur's chief scout, Richard Allen, is in agreement, reasoning that "Scouting is not an exact science." He believes that technical skill is what should be looked for, "It's about trying to beat someone and get the ball past them, not pass it past them, we can all do that."

Yet there has been criticism of targeting players based on their 'skill'. If you find a player already possessing skill then excellent, yet for others - scouts should be looking for a player's movement, decision making and understanding over skill. Dr Richard Bailey, an expert in long term development and talent identification, believes that "The importance of technical proficiency is massively overrated," and that *personality* is the key for talent identification.

> When evaluating technical or physical qualities, we must always remember the critical role that the mind has to play not only for football but across all elite level sport.

MacNamara *et al.* (2010) reported in *The Sport Psychologist* how a range of psychological factors underpin an athlete's ability to translate 'potential' into top-class performance. They noted the findings of Kunst and Florescu who highlighted the role of psychological factors in talent development as early as the 1970's, suggesting that these constructs accounted for over 50% of the variance in development efficacy.

MacNamara and colleagues point out that psychological factors accounted for less than 15% of talent development models at that time, writing "[the] situation does not appear drastically different in the current climate with Talent Identification and Development (TID) models continuing to place limited emphasis on the role of psychological factors and instead employing testing protocols based almost entirely on current performance (e.g., how well an athlete performs at that particular moment in time) or physical/anthropometric characteristics (e.g., how similar they are to 'established norms' for elites."

The research found that determination and persistence, motivation and autonomy are all necessary for "the attainment of excellence by facilitating the acquisition of skills and enabling athletes to invest the requisite time to practice and stay committed to the development process." The researchers stressed that these psychological factors are ignored by the present talent identification models which leave behind individuals who possess the necessary 'personality' for elite performance.

MacNamara's research has found that the difference in individuals who attain excellence is their 'desire' and 'willingness' to persevere and work hard.

Based on these findings - are English academies and scouts putting enough value on a player's personality and character? Are we seeing the failings of English academies because of their focus on the physicality and skill of players over the intelligence and personality of others?

## Ahead of the rest on the south coast

For all the criticism of English academies there is an academy which appears to be ahead of the rest. We have discussed Southampton already – they were among the first clubs to adopt an academy system at the end of the 1990s, when they still were a Premier League club - and it is also important to consider their approach to scouting.

At Southampton they insisted on finding kids possessing intelligence and athleticism. Rupert Lowe put in place a "model that aimed at providing a proper structure to turn out clever players." In an interview with *The Guardian*, Lowe made clear that Southampton's academy searched for players with, "intelligence and athleticism." He pointed out that football ability, "is not necessarily the key at that [academy] age," and that "You can teach them the rest. If they're not clever and not athletic, you'll find it hard to push water uphill."

> It seems likely that personality is the most important aspect of talent identification.

## Summary

English academies need to re-evaluate their talent identification models and start looking at aspects of intelligence and personality over physical strength or height, and possibly even technical skill. A model which assesses a player's intelligence, personality and athletic speed may be the best approach for future recruitment models.

A willingness to learn, work hard, and a drive to succeed will enable a player to overcome setbacks and acquire both game intelligence and technical mastery. It appears evident that personality is vital for the development of professional footballers. If personality is such an important attribute, can it be cultivated and developed like a player's technical skills? As the following chapter will discuss, a player's mindset is, indeed, a most important element for coaches to develop.

# 18

# The Power of The Mind

*"Virtually every success story seen in history involves someone or some group working harder than their peers."* Dan Coyle.

## The key factor in developing footballers

What do top-level athletes all have in common? According to researchers, such as Carol Dweck, the difference between becoming an elite professional and staying an amateur is based on what happens in the mind. Elite performers are able to perform when the pressure is highest and the opposition is strongest. It has to do with their psychology and mindset. Elite athletes have mastered the skill of mental toughness.

Young footballers have many barriers to becoming a professional. Dealing with injury, setbacks and making mistakes can all have a detrimental effect on a player during their developmental years. Being able to train the mind and work on improving a player's mindset has become an important tool in helping young footballers deal with setbacks - allowing them to continue on their journey. As Delice Coffey, a psychologist who specialises in sport argues, "Mental toughness is a learned skill… it is a necessity for all athletes to master and needs to be trained as frequently and seriously as you would train your body physically."

> The psychology of young individuals can be argued to
> be the single most important factor in turning
> a good player into an elite one.

Yet 'sport psychology' has been viewed negatively in English football for decades. Dan Abrahams, the author of *Soccer Tough*, believes the word 'psychology' comes heavily loaded and is perceived (incorrectly) as relating to 'problems' or mental health issues.

According to Abrahams, English football has been restrictive and mistrustful of sports psychology for many years. He believes football suffers from a 'fear of the unknown' yet he also blames the psychologists who are 'fully qualified' but who do not know how to 'sell' the benefits of psychology.

Abrahams believes psychologists can make it too complicated when talking about complex theories - things coaches and footballers don't necessarily want to hear. Abrahams is of the opinion that English football needs to be more open-minded to all performance components because, as this chapter discusses, the power of the mind may be the key to bringing more players through to the professional game.

## Mindset and motivation

When you listen to the world's best players, players such as Lionel Messi and Cristiano Ronaldo, they always talk about their need to improve further, and to keep honing their skills. They never seem to be content and thus continue to improve and be the best.

Imagine if we could make all our players believe that hard work and practice will improve performance - there are no better examples for players than Messi and Ronaldo. How coaches talk to their players, and how they commend them, are key motivators for players to work hard.

Mindset underpins skill and game intelligence, and also mediates how well those qualities are executed on game day. Carol Dweck defines mindset as beliefs, "beliefs about yourself and your most basic qualities."

Anders Ericsson's research shows that most world class experts practice between three and five hours a day, no matter what skill they pursue. This level of training, focus and dedication requires a strong and dedicated mindset and therefore requires a player to maintain high levels of motivation.

The key question, therefore, is how hard are young players willing to work? Are they willing to sacrifice other aspects to their lives, and be disciplined? Do they possess the drive to succeed?

> Pro-academies have an essential role in providing an environment for their players where focus, 'working hard', and challenge are promoted. They must produce a 'deliberate practice' environment.

Now hard work, obsession and winning are all great, but what happens if a player experiences failures or setbacks? Many players cannot deal with this period, where expectations of behaviour and commitment, along with the expectations and pressures of family and friends, can increase the burden and stresses of seeking to become a professional. This is where mindset is tested the most and where many players struggle to achieve their potential. Carol Dweck's work on mindset at Stanford University is opening up coaches', parents' and teachers' eyes to developing young people who deal with failure in a positive way.

# In search of the growth mindset

Motivation is the key aspect of a player's progress and Carol Dweck believes that improvement is all about having young children and adults willing to see times of failure as times of development and learning. Dweck's research has found there are two types of people; those with a 'fixed' mindset and those with a 'growth' mindset. She believes the type of mindset a person has can determine their ability to succeed.

Her research has found that the way children and young athletes are spoken to and, importantly, 'commended' can be a key factor in their development towards becoming an elite athlete. She argues in her book, *Mindset*, that coaches who praise the talented players for their 'abilities', for their 'natural talent', are actually affecting a player's development detrimentally.

The argument goes that when individuals who are successful at tasks are commended in this way, when they eventually find something they cannot perform successfully, they believe that they aren't 'naturally talented' at such a task. Dweck has found that the majority of these individuals will *not* seek to improve their performance; instead they will neglect a task which they cannot do and settle for an easier task which they are successful in, where they will be commended as being 'talented'.

We have discussed already the importance of making mistakes in order to improve, and how essential this is for 'development'. Yet Dweck is finding that certain individuals do not want to make mistakes, or be seen as 'failures'. Ultimately by not 'stretching' themselves and furthering their development the individual will not improve and will not be able to reach improved levels of learning.

It is not hard to see this mindset in English football's culture for decades. Coaches will always tend to compliment and shower platitudes upon the 'talented' players and you will often hear the phrases "you are so talented," or "you're a natural." Dweck believes it is this type of feedback which promotes the 'fixed' mindset. For her, this gives a player the sense they are 'naturally' better than the rest. She believes there is a solution; by simply changing the wording of feedback, coaches could give a player a much better opportunity to progress.

Dweck argues that by praising work rate over talent, a coach can motivate a player or group to persist and overcome boundaries. Players will see mistakes as learning tools and challenges and not as signs of being un-talented.

> As coaches, it is important to improve communication with players to promote a 'growth' mindset.

People who possess the 'growth mindset' have been found to be more willing to challenge and "stretch" themselves. As Dweck says, "This is the mindset that allows people to thrive during some of the most challenging times in their lives." She continues, "When we teach people the growth mindset with its focus on development, those ideas about challenge and effort follow. People in a growth mindset don't just seek challenge, they thrive on it. The bigger the challenge, the more they stretch. And nowhere can it be seen more clearly than in the world of sports."

# Dealing with setbacks

There is an example often used by sports scientists to illustrate the importance of a growth mindset. Michael Jordan is widely regarded as the best basketball player ever, a man with a willingness and drive, combined with immense skill, that brought success to his Chicago Bulls side.

Yet did you know that he was not selected for his Varsity team in high school? At 17, he was not considered good enough. Incredible considering that he is now viewed as one of the greatest athletes of all time. Yet perhaps it was his reaction to this rejection which made Jordan the player he became. The story of Michael Jordan is the epitome of why a growth mindset develops elite performers.

After being rejected, Jordan did not just accept he wasn't good enough; he decided to work on his skills, and enhance his speed and agility, all through hard work and determination. He said, "I think that not making the Varsity team drove me to really work at my game, and also taught me that if you set goals, and work hard to achieve them - the hard work can pay off."

And what about Lionel Messi? He is another world class athlete who proves what can be achieved by overcoming setbacks and disappointment. At 11 years old Messi had a problem; he was informed that he would not grow to a 'normal' height unless he was given a growth hormone treatment. This was costly and all the clubs in Argentina were not willing to pay for these injections. At this point he must have thought his dreams of being like his idol, Maradona, were over.

Those feelings as a young 11-year-old, being told he that he would not grow properly and that clubs in Argentina did not want him, must have devastated the young Messi. Yet he chose to stay in the game, and Barcelona subsequently took a risk on the young player after seeing him play. What a gamble it has proved to be. They were willing to pay for the injections which he needed and we are seeing their investment pay off today. Messi did not allow those rejections and setbacks to knock him back and stop his dream; he persevered, remained strong, and ultimately proved himself worth the investment.

Messi highlighted how mental toughness and his desire overcame his setbacks. That kind of mindset is what separates the best from the rest. Imagine if it had all been plain sailing for Messi. Would he be the player he is today? It is doubtful.

> Obstacles and setbacks may be required to force a player to work harder - to prevent them coasting.

# Being released - rejection or a challenge?

As the story of Messi proves, the career of a young footballer is not always easy and straightforward. So when we consider the issue of players being released from academies at sixteen, we must see the situation as a challenge, and a test, and not failure. As York City's academy director, Tony Mee, says, "I challenge every player that we ever release to come back and rub our noses in it! Nothing would give me greater satisfaction."

Rejection may be the necessary jolt to push talent forward. Take Callum McManaman. By all accounts Callum McManaman was the top player in his group between the ages of 12 and 14 at Everton's academy. He was touted as having the potential to be 'as good as Rooney'. High praise for a young player, as you can imagine. Yet, by sixteen years of age, Everton did not think McManaman had the attributes necessary for professional football, or at least to play for Everton, and they released him.

This decision to let McManaman go was perhaps the key reason for his professional career today. That rejection re-focused him and made him realise that he needed to do more. He worked hard and proved himself worthy of a contract at Wigan. In the FA Cup final he would receive the man of the match award for his impressive display. McManaman worked hard to prove those who doubted him wrong.

This idea of 'proving others wrong' epitomises one of England's finest ever players. As a young teenager Steven Gerrard was invited to the national football school at Lilleshall (a place we discussed in Part I). Being selected to attend this school was a big deal for young players and Gerrard was very excited about it. However, although he performed well in the trials, he was not selected. As he says in his autobiography "Never before had someone dared tell me I was not up to scratch. Never. My first setback hurt like hell."

Now the funny part of Gerrard's failure to make it at Lilleshall was because he was considered 'small for his age', which neatly illustrates the issues of England's past. Yet the experience may have been necessary for Gerrard. His initial tears turned into a steely resolve which made Gerrard into the player we all know. He suffered much heartache after being rejected yet it intensified his game and his desire. It was perhaps the single most important part of Gerrard's youth development. If he had been selected would he have had the desire to work harder and, as he says, "prove them wrong"?

Reading the above, it is important to consider the importance of a young player having a strong support network. Between 14 and 21 years especially, the resolve to sacrifice things outside football and develop strong levels of discipline are key to 'making it' as a professional. Unfortunately too many talented players lose their focus, become arrogant, or fail to accept that the path to becoming a professional requires more than just attending training. During times of difficulty, or 'failure', a young player requires key people around them to guide, instruct, help, support and importantly keep the player balanced.

A strong support network may be vital for a player to continue to progress and stay focused. Gareth Bale, who is regarded as one of the best players in the world, overcame injuries and struggles in his early career because of his mindset and the support around him.

As he said in an interview with *The Daily Telegraph*, "I had injuries when I was younger, so there have been bad experiences, but you try to use them in a positive way, try to make yourself a bit stronger mentally and physically. It's all about belief.

I've got a good team around me – my agent, my family – and that gave me a lot of confidence going through that time."

Setbacks, failures or rejection can feel like the end of a player's career. Yet, at some point, every player will experience negative emotions. What is important is how a player reacts and perceives 'rejection'. Many will take it negatively and decide to leave football, yet for others - if they possess the right mindset – they can find their way back. It may just be a different path than expected.

# The English mentality

Clearly the right mindset is important for a player's development through the system and this is why coaches and psychologists who can develop this attitude in their players will make a big difference. Yet, allied with a positive growth mindset, it is important for us to consider the aspect we spoke of in the previous chapter, a player's personality.

We discussed how scouts should look at the personality of a player over other 'football' related capabilities because it has been shown that those with a strong, hardworking personality are more likely to make it through the challenging and difficult road of the development pathway.

Unfortunately there are too many players in English academies, particularly between the ages of 16 and 18 (when they become 'scholars') who simply don't have the right attitude to becoming a professional. The sense is that these players think they have 'made it' already, and instead of striving to improve they become arrogant, disrespectful and stop trying, almost like they don't need to make the effort anymore. How ludicrous and damaging for their careers.

In those key years too many players lose their drive and dedication to work harder and improve and wonder why they are not offered a professional contract. We can make allowances for these players by blaming coaches and philosophies but ultimately it is down to the player on how much 'he wants it' and how hard he is willing to work to achieve his goal.

> Too many players are not willing to put in the required work to become a professional.

This can be termed the *English mentality*; it is becoming more common in young people who believe they are 'entitled' without having to put in the work to earn it. Social development, leadership, ownership and responsibility are essential in the tough world of football. Yet too often coaches and parents do too much for the players; they glorify them, pick up for them, answer for them, and simply prevent these players from taking 'responsibility' for their actions and themselves. It can therefore be no surprise that clubs go abroad looking for both more talented and harder working professional players.

Let us look at Spain and their belief in the importance of personality. Andy Roxburgh believes that Spanish players portray 'humility' better than any other nation and their success is actually built on it. "The Barca players are noted for their humility and it shows in the work-rate and the way they behave to other people. That all comes from the youth programme. In Spain, if you're not humble and don't work hard and don't have a family ethic they just don't want you," said Roxburgh in an interview with Henry Winter of *The Daily Telegraph*.

Everton manager Roberto Martinez, who knows the English game well, echoed Roxburgh's sentiments, "Ability on its own is not enough; it's the one who's the better professional who gets through." In Martinez's opinion, "We make it too easy in England. In Spain if a player does a mistake he's out. It's such a competitive environment. Between 16 and 19 they might show you what they can be as players but really the ones who are going to win games and be successful pros are the consistent characters."

The belief is that English players have it too easy in their upbringing as young players. There is a truth in this. If coaches and parents raised the standards of professionalism, character, and respect more - perhaps English football could develop more players capable of being professional. Yes, players must look at themselves and their approach, yet coaches, academies and parents need to be harder on these young men in order to keep them focused and humble.

## Summary

If we are serious about developing elite footballers who can compete with the best in the world then we must seek to use all disciplines open to us. Sport psychology has started to become more accepted both with senior players and with professional academies and many are waking up to the understanding that sport psychology is a valuable tool to further the development of football players of all ages.

Sport psychology can help with play on the pitch also. Dan Abrahams points towards how it can help improve a player's cognitive skills of anticipation, pattern recognition, decision making and awareness - which can ultimately help raise technical and tactical abilities.

Many clubs are beginning to implement psychological testing on their players from 12 onwards in order to understand their players, how they can be motivated, and to gauge the best way to communicate with them. A coach with 16 players will encounter various different styles of learning and motivation. For each individual to achieve success, the coach will need to tailor his approach and having a greater knowledge and understanding of individual players will certainly help.

It is also important that parents and grassroots coaches are aware of the impact that their communication has on their players. Young players are heavily influenced by those around them and those people need to be more aware of the impact of their words.

It is clear that sport psychology and the 'right' communication can offer young footballers the skills needed to overcome periods of failure and disappointment as well as helping facilitate higher levels of success. Evidently, psychology can be the difference between a player becoming a professional, or not, and more of these experts are needed across English academies.

# Part IV

# England's Future

# 19

# The Aftermath of Euro 2000

*"For a long time we have been 'asleep' at youth level, we now have new concepts."*
Matthias Sammer, former German Football Association (DFB) technical director.

## Learning from failure

At the European Championships in 2000, Germany and England were drawn in the same group, along with Portugal and Romania. It would be a tournament to forget for both nations, Germany earned one point and England three, with a win against Germany. It was a disappointing tournament and a first round exit materialised for both teams. It was clear that something was wrong. The manner of the performances highlighted a lack of quality, poor coaching, and - like every tournament - opened up questions into the 'state of the game'.

England simply felt a change of manager at the top would suffice, after all this was the beginning of the era of the 'Golden Generation' - how could the failings be the players? In fact, as we have discussed already, problems arose due to *both manager and players*, yet England failed to address the underlying issue of player development. Germany, however, sought to address the foundations of their game and a decade on - we are seeing the fruits of their labours.

Howard Wilkinson had foreseen the issues plaguing youth development in 1997 and had offered his observations and guidance for the future. Yet these were mostly ignored or watered down. His proposals could have been great for English football's future; instead we endured a depressing decade of disappointment on the international stage.

> England has continued to fail to address young players' deficiencies and those of the country's coaches.

Only now has England 'woken-up' to the realisation that something should have been done at the foundation level of English football. Now, as the Golden Generation comes to a finale, we find we have a national group devoid of experience and high quality. England is further away from the top nations than even before.

## The German efficiency model

Following Euro 2000, the German FA looked at why their team failed and concluded that there were not enough young players with the necessary qualities to make the German national team great. It was only four years earlier that Germany had won Euro 1996, in England, yet there were some serious questions being asked of that team and the future. This 'new generation' appeared to be lacking the necessary attributes for the contemporary game.

So what did they do? For Germany, the years following Euro 2000 were about investing in youth development and changing philosophies; the DFB (German Football Association) wanted to move away from playing in straight lines and relying on 'the German mentality' to win matches. The key aspects that would help them on their new project were to employ more full-time coaches and to upgrade their facilities.

Germany has always valued coaching and had a vast number of trained coaches *before* the new model was put in place, yet what was significant was that all these coaches were educated in the 'new way'. Thus Germany had thousands of expertly trained coaches focused on German football's future.

121 national talent centres were built in order to help 10 to 17-year-olds with technical and tactical coaching. Each centre would employ two full-time coaches that, as Robin Dutt, the former sporting director of the DVB, made clear: were instructed to focus on, "…developing fluid formations that required the sort of nimble, dexterous players who would previously have been overlooked because of their lack of physical strength."

These centres were, as Stuart James pointed out in *The Guardian*, aided by a talent development programme which was set up by the DFB in 2003 with "the aim of identifying promising youngsters and providing them with technical skills and tactical knowledge at an early age." Covering 366 areas of Germany, players aged 8 to 14 were 'scouted', and as Dutt says, "We have 80 million people in Germany and I think, before 2000, nobody noticed a lot of talent. Now we notice everyone."

The DFB also made it a requirement for all 36 professional clubs in the Bundesliga and Bundesliga 2 to build youth academies and with this came perhaps the most significant change in Germany. These new academies were instructed that at least 12 players in each intake were to be eligible to play for Germany. This requirement enabled home grown youth players to play more, allowing them to gain the necessary experience to improve.

So let us just highlight what Germany did and what England failed to do. Investment in coaching, a change of philosophy, improved scouting methods and investment in facilities. And now a decade later German football is being talked of as the best in world football and the 'model' on which others should follow. The German youth development model was based on long term sustainability and the decade has been one of patience for German football. Like Spain's success it has come from addressing the root issues which are youth development and coaching.

The German approach has meant it is not a few teams who have benefitted but all of them. Standards have improved, players developed more, and after 13 years they have a successful national team and a football culture whose foundations are built on expert planning, a modern philosophy, and great coaching.

> Germany's success has involved educating and developing expert coaches and having them go work in development centres around the country.

# Working together

Germany's 're-emergence' on the world scene came at the European Under-21 tournament in 2009 when the German team showed everyone watching that the country was in the process of producing world class players and teams for the future. They destroyed an average England in the final, 4-0, and gave credence to the long term development plan put in place after 2000.

At the 2010 World Cup England were shown up again by an excellent counter attacking team possessing fast, creative and clinical players in an organised German team which won 4-1. This team possessed players from that Under-21 side, most notably Mesut Ozil. German football's production line was in full swing and the world was made aware that Germany had would be challenging for honours for the next decade.

Although the DFB don't 'tell' the clubs what to do, it appears that the philosophies and principles which were created a decade ago are used throughout Germany's academies. German football is very much working together when it comes to developing youth. As Dutt said in, the German paper *Der Tagesspiegel*, "We want to network at all levels so that we have in Germany a few technical and tactical principles. Just as we once had the German virtues as a trademark, so we now want to do with tempo and counter pressing, combination football in a small space a new identity."

Dutt views the work of the clubs in Germany as helping the national team and so the idea of a conflict is not evident, as he says, "If we help the clubs, we help us, because the players of our national teams – the youth teams and Joachim Löw's team – come from the clubs."

It is a great example of German efficiency; a plan was put in place and through far sighted planning and co-operation between federations and clubs a new generation was produced.

This is the opposite to what happens in England, where the FA has little influence on clubs to develop youngsters and where clubs look at taking the 'best players' regardless of nationality. This is where, and why, England is failing to produce more talented players.

> Both Germany's national team and domestic clubs
> have benefited from an emphasis on youth development
> and nurturing potential stars.

# England's corporate greed

German football has always valued domestic talent and has not had a lot of foreign managers in their top league. This comes in part because of the relatively low television money and, of course, the rule which prevents a Roman Abramovich type figure owning a club outright.

The German model of club ownership is the 50+1 rule where a minimum of 51% of the club must be owned by club members. This still allows for considerable investment opportunities for private business yet prevents them from having overall control of the direction of the club. As Tim Dobson explains, "A Bundesliga club board is made up of delegates selected by the shareholders. That way the supporter membership associations have a direct say on the management of the club."

Hans Joachim Watzke, the chief executive of Dortmund, says clubs like his ensure fans feel a part of the club by involving them as members. He believes the English ownership model results in fans being treated as clients and has 'killed the romance of the game'.

English clubs' success this past decade has not been built on top coaching education or great youth development but predominantly thanks to foreign managers and players. Money has allowed these clubs to import talent instead of developing their own.

English football is suffering because corporate interest reduces the involvement and impact of the supporters. German clubs don't allow corporate greed to affect the vision and philosophy of their clubs and as long as the supporters have the best interest of the club at heart, that club is unlikely to allow itself to become mismanaged. Therefore it is little surprise that Germany's clubs value the national team as they are controlled by German nationals.

The Premier League is restricting England's chances at achieving success because they are not being strong enough on clubs developing home grown talent. The overreliance on foreign players has decreased the opportunities offered to home grown talent with the resultant knock-on effect for the England national team.

Until the governing bodies in England agree (and enforce) that clubs have to have more English players in their teams, then the national team will not improve.

In England there is a strong case to be made that we should follow the German model of youth development, and their values, to underpin our development pathways. After all, England resembles Germany more than any other country in terms of style, attitude and characteristics.

> The English Premier League has become too corporate,
> being run by men who appear to have little, or no,
> regard for the national game.

## Summary

The truth is that English football has been going through a crisis for decades. The vast amount of money pouring into the game has allowed English club sides to remain competitive over the past decade but other countries have shown up England at the international level and highlighted English football's failings.

Compared to nations like Germany, Spain and Holland, England are very much lagging behind. Investment in youth development, coach education, and importantly a style of football which suits the modern game have enabled other nations to excel. England has suffered because of a lack of vision, a lack of communication and broken relationships between the clubs and governing bodies which have restricted growth. English needs to be managed much better in the future if it wishes to improve.

# 20
# The FA's Priorities

*"That is going to be one of the big challenges. How do we get talented kids, properly coached, into the top level of English football?"* Greg Dyke, Chairman of the English FA.

## Experience is the key ingredient

English football has entered that most dreaded of times, the stage of 'transition'. It is a time of flux and the words 'hope' and 'future' are used widely and often. Frequently, this means that the present is filled with negativity and failure.

An overreliance on the Golden Generation has seen a decade of limited opportunity for England's younger players with the key experiences of international football on the back foot. England has suffered in each tournament yet they have also failed to plan for the future because the same players kept getting taken to tournaments. Each competition has seen a larger chasm between the best countries and England emerge. As the Golden Generation comes to an inglorious end, English football has been exposed as being in crisis.

England's manager, Roy Hodgson, has inherited a group of players who are in serious need of international and top club level experience - yet who lack it in abundance. Why do England's young players lack so much experience? It mainly has to do with the English arrogance shown towards international youth sides, and the fast-tracking of talented young players.

A key opportunity for young players to gain experience and knowledge of international football is through tournaments. At the 2011 UEFA European Under-

21 tournament England made of a mockery of their participation, and it was a key indicator that we simply do not value players gaining experience. The coach Stuart Pearce was adamant that England's top young players should have gone to the tournament, yet too many dropped out.

In the more recent 2013 tournament the same thing happened once again. England came to the competition with players who, for the most part, were devoid of any Premier League experience. Effectively it was a Championship Under-21 team. The result was inevitable and England exited at the group stage for the second time running. Where were the Premier League youngsters? England has a habit of 'fast tracking' talented youngsters through the youth system straight up to the senior side; it prevents these players from experiencing tournaments and competitive games and gaining crucial tournament know-how.

Surely those who are eligible to play for the Under-21 side should represent their country in a tournament such as the Euros? At the time of the 2013 tournament, it was quite ludicrous to see a friendly versus Brazil (in Brazil) as more important than an actual competition. Yet that is what happened with players such as Alex Oxlade-Chamberlain, Jack Rodwell and Phil Jones playing at the Maracana, Rio de Janeiro.

> No wonder we struggle in tournaments, our young players are not used to them.

Players should be playing throughout their age groups to experience tournament play and the feeling of the 'big games'. At the 2008 Olympics, Argentina's Lionel Messi and Sergio Aguero both represented their country. Not only was it an honour for them, they won gold and they are now two of the best players in the world. *These* world class players were not 'above' playing for their country's 'youth' side.

Spain's Cesc Fabregas and Germany's Mesut Ozil all gained their first experience of international tournaments at Under-21 level. Were these experiences key to their rise to the top? It certainly would have helped.

Spain is a great example here. They have won almost every tournament worth winning these past several years and were once again crowned Under-21 European champions in 2013. The fact is, Spain has understood the key methods of youth development through their coaching, style and philosophy. They also respect and understand how tournament football for their youth sides is not only important for players to experience particular games and environments but also for building team cohesion over the coming decade.

The bonds built and the knowledge gained from top level tournaments, and the relationships built between players on and off the pitch, laid the foundation for the side we see today. Players like Iker Casillas, Sergio Ramos, Carlos Puyol, Xavi, Iniesta, and David Villa, the spine of the successful national side over the past few years developed and grew up together through the youth sides. When Spain plays, player understanding is as strong as for many club sides. It is therefore unsurprising that the Spanish team appears to know each other's movements, intentions and positions more than many international sides.

The worry for England has always been the neglect or even disdain shown to youth competitions, where many players (often with club pressure) will choose not to travel and represent their country, believing themselves to be too good for that level or preserving themselves for the more important season ahead with their club.

This is not conducive to a winning side. English football needs to see the value in playing for all levels of the national side and put more into winning tournaments and building 'cohesion' at Under-17, 19, and 21 levels.

# The beast which is the Premier League

The 'inexperience' of top level football for many young English players has one major culprit. At the close of the 1991 season, a proposal for the establishment of a new league was tabled that would bring more money into the game overall. The Founder Members Agreement, signed on 17 July 1991, by the game's top-flight clubs, established the basic principles for setting up the FA Premier League.

The newly formed top division would have commercial independence from The Football Association and the Football League, giving the FA Premier League licence to negotiate its own broadcast and sponsorship agreements. The argument given at the time was that the extra income would allow English clubs to compete with teams across Europe and that the league would *also benefit the national team*.

Yet as the new deal for 2013-2016 is inked and now worth £5 billion - the England national team appears still further away from competing with the world's best, and the truth is that the Premier League has damaged English football.

We have seen the emergence of foreign owners coming into the game which has propelled the finances and splendour of the league. The increased transfer fees and high wages have brought in more talent, yet it has come at a cost.

For all the 'advantages' that foreign owners and players bring, we have a league filled with 60% overseas players who are restricting the development of home grown English talent due to the demands of instant success.

# The FA's role

If the FA had been the one 'in power' would we have seen improved standards and a better national team? For well over a century the English FA has been responsible for coaching and development standards. Yet, one could argue convincingly, their methods have failed to produce the necessary quality in home grown coaching and playing talent: a lack of vision, a disastrous philosophy, and poor planning illustrate how the FA has failed the country for decades.

The concern that many coaches have, is that they cannot 'trust' the English FA to put in place a philosophy and style which is conducive for English football to develop players and teams for the modern game.

Admittedly, in 2009, the FA produced *The Future Game* – a document which pointed to what the modern game would involve for players and teams. However, it was put forward as a guideline, not a requirement. The English FA should have been more forthright in their approach to improving the national style and making sure more coaches and teams across the country played and developed in a modern style.

> Charles Hughes' philosophy still plagues people's beliefs towards the FA and they have not done anything drastic to change that opinion of them.

# The FA needs to stand up

It has been argued that one problem with the FA is that it has not been run by football people but by businessmen who value commercial interests over their role as developers of the game. There certainly appear to be too many people afraid of change at the FA and this has held English football back. Howard Wilkinson and Trevor Brooking have both been loud proponents for change, for over a decade, yet their calls for change have largely been ignored.

Perhaps changes are afoot with the arrival of the new FA chairman Greg Dyke. Dyke, the ex-Director General of the BBC, bluntly admitted the influx of money and foreign stars has come at the expense of England's national side. He said, in the *Daily Mail*, "We have a situation where English football, by and large at the top level, is owned overseas, is managed by people from overseas and played by people from overseas. It's turned it into a brilliant league, but it does give a problem with the English team."

Dyke sees it as his role to ensure more English players start coming through; as the quote at the top of the chapter says, "That is going to be one of the big challenges (for me). How do we get talented kids, properly coached, into the top level of English football?"

Dyke's first job may be to consider the criticism The FA have recently received. They have been criticised by the government for their failure to introduce new financial controls or to increase the influence of fans. The Culture, Media and Sport Select Committee accused the Football Association, the Premier League and the Football League of a "very disappointing" response to its report published in July 2011, which followed a wide-ranging inquiry into the governance of the game.

Allied to renewed concerns over home-grown talent, following an abject showing at the 2010 World Cup, the embarrassing failure of the bid to host the 2018 World Cup, and longstanding concerns about the dysfunctional structure of the FA – the Sports Minister, Hugh Robertson, was prompted to say that, "Football is the worst governed sport in this country, without a doubt."

The report wanted the FA to "restructure its main board to assert its independence, overhaul the FA Council to make it more representative, introduce tough new rules on financial regulation, and increase the influence of supporters on how their clubs were run."

The select committee has urged the FA to 'reform its structure'. As the committee says, "We urge the authorities to be more radical and more urgent in addressing the problems faced by the game because of the weaknesses in its governance structure, both at FA and club level."

They believe that a "fundamental overhaul of the FA council" is needed to help the FA improve standards and modernise the English game. They believe that the council lacks "diversity" yet this is not hard to understand when you consider that the council has 118 members, many of whom have served for more than 20 years and two-thirds of them are aged 64 or over. Clearly, the FA is in need of a change because, at this time, English football in the hands of the wrong people. The FA needs a radical shakeup in order to improve standards and the future of the English game.

Clearly, Greg Dyke has a lot to do.

## Proof is in action, not words

Perhaps the FA cannot influence the 'machine' which is the Premier League yet they should look upon their role as leaders of the grassroots game with more drive and determination. There are significant issues which need addressing at the key phase of youth football. It is the foundation where the building blocks for future successes are laid.

St George's Park, the new training centre at Burton, cost £100 million to build. It was opened in 2012 yet plans were in place in 2002 and building started in 2003. By 2006 funding was cut so that the FA could invest their time and money in building the new Wembley. This alone highlights where the FA's priorities lie.

The FA has invested almost a billion pounds into the new Wembley. Yet did we need to build a new national stadium? We could have followed the Germans, where there is no national stadium; games of the national team are always in different cities. This allows more people to see their team and allows more money to be put into key areas.

Imagine where the £900 million spent on Wembley could have gone? If the FA was serious about improving the standards of youth development we could have seen 80-100 'development centres' run by the FA Skills programme, right across the country, which would have meant more youth coaches and players being developed.

That money could also have gone into subsidising coaching courses which could have meant more investment in developing a greater number of 'quality' coaches.

The FA cannot say they do not have the money, what they do not have is the *desire* to make significant changes at the foundation level. Too much money at the top trying to fix problems that need addressing at the bottom.

> The FA has a major responsibility to make sure every player is given the opportunity to receive good coaching which is inclusive and enjoyable as well as positive for a player's development.

## Where's the investment?

Dan Roan, of BBC Sports News, looked into the 'investment' which the FA is making at the grassroots level and came up with some worrying findings. He makes the point that, "at a time when the onus on boosting the numbers playing the sport has never been greater, the amount of money being put into grassroots facilities is being reduced."

He found that from its original commitment of £20m per annum, the FA currently gives £12m; a mere fraction of its income. For Roan "The governing body's contribution to the entire country's grassroots facilities appears far from generous." He also makes the case against the Premier League which is gaining from a £5.1bn television broadcasting rights deal but investing just £12m into the grassroots each year.

The Premier League also gives £20.3m to clubs' community and social inclusion schemes, £3m internationally, and £8.1m to the Football League for community work and youth development. But it still represents small beer compared to the vast broadcasting income it generates.

Roan argues that, "A lack of investment in high quality facilities has left the UK behind nations such as Holland, Germany, France and Spain and this is evident in the players we produce."

## Summary

There is no doubt that the Premier League has taken control of English football and left the FA very much playing second fiddle. The league is proving hugely valuable and beneficial for clubs and their shareholders yet it is not helping the development of domestic players.

Proof is in action and it appears abundantly clear where the focus and interest of the FA and the Premier League lies. This is a real shame for the future of the English game, especially for those with an interest in youth development.

The FA needs to stand up and do more to improve standards at the foundation level where they can exert more control and direction over coaches and players. What is needed is a visionary approach followed by forward planning; it's essential if our game is to survive.

Other nations have a clear philosophy and vision of what they wish to produce and develop in their national game from youth to the seniors, and the English FA needs to do more in this respect. Our national body needs to improve its strategic thinking and be more courageous in its future planning and investment. Yes, St George's Park is now open, but can one national football centre really be the change which England needs?

# 21

# St George's Legacy

*"I think we're in a good place. I hope that we've done enough. This is the next 15 to 20 years of youth football we're talking about here."* Nick Levett.

## A breakthrough for youth development

May 28th, 2012, was a landmark day for youth football in England. It was the day that youth development proposals were approved by the FA which included a revised player pathway focused on small-sided football, and new 5v5 and 9v9 formats up to the Under-12's age group.

For the first time ever in English football, children will only begin to play on full size pitches once they reach Under-13 level. Amazingly, there have been young children who have been playing 11v11 on full size adult pitches, with goalkeepers playing in full size adult goals. As well as the changes in team size, for teams up to the Under-11's, the traditional league format will be replaced by three six-week 'trophy events', allowing all teams to play 'competitive' football for 18 weeks of a 26 week season, rather than competing for a single league trophy over an entire season.

For Nick Levett, the FA's National Development Manager for Youth and Mini Soccer, and the man behind the proposals, the AGM vote represented the final hurdle of a two-and-a half-year project featuring extensive research and a nationwide consultation procedure. The reforms have brought praise from Howard Wilkinson, "The most exciting and aspirational piece of work that he'd seen the FA do in years." High praise and clearly these changes are showing a positive change for the English grassroots game.

> With the new changes being implemented, English
> football may be on the cusp of a revolution
> in terms of youth development.

The reforms have the potential to put in place a future where youth football can be progressed for the good of the players *and* the national side over the coming decades. Yet, we have been here before with Wilkinson's Charter, and it was no surprise that the term 'watered down' was mentioned as this proposal was ratified.

That being said, this still represented the biggest change to youth football since the introduction of mini soccer in 1999.

As we have spoken of, throughout this book, players *need* to play games in order to develop their skills and intelligence. With the new rules changing the number of players in the younger age groups, and the restriction on the size of the pitches, we should see more players getting more touches, developing their skills, and improving. But there are more issues to address if we want to develop players for the elite game.

## One building is not enough

Each international tournament brings about the same issues and concerns about the national side; namely how little changes each time. While Spain sought to improve their standards in the 1990's and Germany saw their own failings in 2000, England continually 'sees' the problems yet has continually failed to address the issue.

It is felt that the new national football centre will be the catalyst for England's future. And yet it is hard not to believe that this is just going to be another false dawn.

A new building is not going to change the development of our players. The real changes will come from the quality of coaching that young players receive across the country, from P.E. in schools, to the grassroots level, and onto the elite academies. The key for England's future is to improve the foundations of youth development. Quality coaching will make this happen but the question is - are our coaches good enough to develop our young footballers?

We have blamed Premier League clubs for looking for talent elsewhere yet the truth is that too many of our players are not good enough. Clubs are looking abroad for talented players because we, as a nation, are not developing players capable of competing with the best in the world.

> If we don't improve our standards, if we don't strive
> and aim for excellence and move away from
> accepting mediocrity, then we won't have
> a chance of producing world class players.

# English football's most important role

A need for improved standards in the game is a necessity. And the man to make this happen is the newly appointed Technical Director of The FA.

This position can be said to matter more to the development of England than any other. Howard Wilkinson was the only previous permanent incumbent and that was a decade ago. Amazingly, since Wilkinson quit the post in 2002, to manage Sunderland, only Les Reed has performed the function on a temporary basis for two years afterwards. This means that English football's development plan has been running on pretty much 'auto-pilot' for a decade. No wonder we have not moved forwards.

The role of the Technical Director is to work and focus on the important issues that will improve the standard of the national game. Therefore it was a surprise to many people when the FA chose Dan Ashworth for the role as the FA's 'Director of Elite Development'.

Dan Ashworth is not a name well known by many in football yet he may be the most important man the FA has appointed in decades. Previously Ashworth was West Bromwich Albion's sporting and technical director and impressed Roy Hodgson when he was manager at the club. He arrived at West Bromwich Albion in 2004 to work at the club's academy and progressed through the ranks due to his impressive coaching and personal approach.

In December 2007, Ashworth was appointed as the club's sporting and technical director and he has been the brains behind Albion's renaissance in recent years, transforming the academy set-up, recruiting astutely at senior level, and working closely with the head coaches. He was headhunted for the role at the FA because of what he achieved at West Brom, the hope being that he can replicate his success at the FA. In his role, Ashworth will be working with Trevor Brooking and will be involved in developing the country's elite talent, managing the FA's coach education team, and ensuring that the facilities at St George's Park are used efficiently.

The concern, however, is whether this appointment points towards improvement or the continuation of mediocrity. The German FA was propelled forward by the experience of Matthias Sammer, the ex-Germany and Dortmund captain. Spain has excelled through the work of ex-Spain and Real Madrid captain Fernando Hierro who was sporting director between 2007 and 2011.

Ashworth, however, is a risk in terms of his experience. Would Steve McLaren or Glenn Hoddle have been better options for the role? Perhaps. Unfortunately, their 'poisoned chalice' work as managers of England has affected their chances of working with the FA. Yes, Ashworth is a risk, but he may be a better option than Gareth Southgate or Stuart Pearce.

> The technical director can be said to occupy the most important and influential role at the English FA.

# Developing modern coaches

There is no doubt that coaching has become more technical and precise, and the truth is that English football is not equipped for the modern game right now. While we have sat idly by - nations like Spain, Germany and Belgium have been busy improving youth development.

Dan Ashworth's role is simple: to modernise the teaching and philosophy of football in England. We are seeing already that as the game evolves, players' roles and positions are becoming more fluid and flexible. We are amazed when we see foreign players move from their positional 'role' and then wonder how they find such time and space. They are modern players and we need to produce a new generation of players like this. We cannot just have one per generation - like Hoddle, Scholes, Rooney or Wilshere. English football needs to produce more players with craft, vision, movement, and game understanding.

To do so, England must move away from developing fixed positions which offer no variation or creativity. If we wish for a future of 'fluidity' then we need players who can play these roles - we need to produce players who are 'universal', players who possess the necessary technical, tactical, physical and psychological skills to be capable of playing in different positions on the pitch. It will be up to the new generation of coaches to teach them.

> Ashworth and the FA need to develop intelligent coaches who can then produce intelligent players.

# Football's future

As coaches we must seek to *anticipate* how the game will change at the highest level and lead the way. The game of the future will become much faster both with, and without, the ball. As space and time is reduced the future player will have less time on the ball, less time between passes, and will need fewer touches. Player movement, decision making, and technical skill will need to be extremely high to cope with the demands of the game. Tactical nous will become a requirement not a bonus.

We hope that the FA, under Dan Ashworth, will make the improvements needed for our national game. Yet the truth is we, as coaches, cannot sit and wait for a governing body which has failed to deliver for decades. Real change will come from ourselves and what *we* do. Our young footballers look to us to teach them skills, make them better players, and allow them to be creative. The future is in our hands, this is a massive responsibility and it is one we should take real pride in. What a role we have!

# 22

# Solutions for England's Future

In this final chapter we will look at the solutions which need to be implemented if English football is to grow stronger in the future. The outlook for English football can be positive if we seek to address the issues discussed in this book. If we make improvements across all areas then how can we not improve the quality of our players and teams?

## Solution 1 – Investment in school sport

As we focus on football we need to address what we can do to create more high quality players. If we wish to improve the standards of our young footballers then we need to start with the foundation of *learning*. Physical literacy is a vital component of any sport: the ability to run and turn and cut. Agility, balance and co-ordination are basic elements for football players. These skills should be learnt at school, through P.E., yet it appears that these lessons are not being taught effectively.

Primary schools are suffering from a lack of quality P.E. teachers and unfortunately many of the outside coaches, who come in to schools, are not highly enough qualified to give young children the necessary physical education. If this continues then children have little opportunity for physical development before 11 years of age.

As schools play such a key role in the development of children's physical literacy - the government needs to invest in school sport and particularly in expert sport teachers in primary schools and lay strong physical foundations for young children.

A joint approach between the government and the Youth Sports Trust would lead to improved levels of physical education in schools so that children from 5-11 would receive a multi-linear development programme of mobility and key multi-skills. If a child *only* plays football and nothing else, then they will develop uni-linear skills which will ultimately stunt their development and restrict their long term mobility.

> If a child is given the right learning environment to learn multiple skills, then they will develop a broader range of skills with a greater potential to progress across multiple sports. Investment in specialist P.E. teachers in primary schools is a necessity.

# Solution 2 – Investment in facilities

England trails other nations like Holland, Spain and Germany for investment into sports facilities around the country. If we wish to develop more talented footballers then we need to give them a greater number of facilities in order to provide them with the environments to flourish.

We have spoken about the 'death of street soccer' and the negative effects that has had on the development of young footballers. This loss of 'free play' and practice time has restricted the development of children's decision making, for the simple reason that the child, in structured games and coaching sessions, is restricted and denied from selecting options. This applies not just to the game itself, but the rules, dimensions, and time.

If children cannot experience 'street soccer' then we need to create ways of providing them with the right opportunities and guidance to improve their skill development; the 7-11 window of opportunity is vital for laying down the foundations of technical excellence.

The solution to this is simple. If children are not allowed to play in the streets anymore then local councils need to invest in building small sided football 'cages' similar to what is seen in Spain and Brazil. The growing popularity of futsal can aid the future development of players and these cages can be a great environment for players to practice their skills. More futsal cages across communities can be the modern version of 'street soccer'.

As well as the creation of 'football cages', schools and councils need to make their own sports facilities accessible at inexpensive prices. Schools are closed thirteen weeks of the year and yet you rarely see their facilities in use. This is a waste.

> Investment in new facilities, as well as a reduction
> in costs for current facilities, is needed to
> give young players a place to 'play'.

# Solution 3 – Develop a national playing style

Dan Ashworth's role at the FA will be to develop a national playing style through which grassroots coaches can develop players. The FA needs to cement a long-term player development strategy and make available a core national coaching syllabus to assist clubs.

For too long the FA has failed to create an all-embracing 'philosophy' for youth development in the way Germany, Spain and Holland have done over the past decades. There needs to be a core coaching strategy aimed at delivering talented young English players to the national teams. How can coaches be taught, and players produced to play, without first establishing a suitable national playing style? A national style template would allow the building blocks to be laid – we know teams should include individual skills but we don't produce appropriate players so we import them. Not a healthy prospect for our football future.

The new youth modules are very good at teaching coaches to develop a positive learning environment yet more could be done to teach the importance of the FA Skills programme, and a style of play for coaches to implement in their small-sided games.

If Ashworth can develop a national playing style which focuses on the development of technically confident and skilful players in possession, as well as tactically efficient individuals (both in and out of possession), then the future can be brighter for English football. The FA needs to make sure coaches are producing more creative players.

We have seen that the most successful club sides adopt a way of playing that is insisted upon from the youngest youth players to the first-team. The vision and philosophy put forward must be effectively communicated at all levels of the game in order to achieve political and professional support.

A recommendation would be to look at educating coaches on the use of a three man midfield in a 4-3-3 or 4-2-3-1 formation. The use of 4-3-3 in youth teams has benefited Ajax, Barcelona, and has been introduced with great success in Belgium this past decade. And it is not just at 11v11 where this can be introduced, the style and philosophy of this formation can be adapted to suit the new small sided formats easily - vital for the development of more creative players.

> The FA must develop a style of playing which can
> be taught to coaches of youth players. It must be
> in line with the needs of the modern game.

# Solution 4 – Developing a coaching culture

Following on from the development of a national playing style it is clear that, in England, the majority of coaching is still very amateur. Archaic training and development sessions are still regularly used.

The truth is that English football lacks an ingrained coaching culture. Football coaching is not viewed with enough respect by many and this has led to it being seen as a 'hobby' more than an actual occupation. This attitude needs to change. Great coaching is required to develop better footballers and also 'good people' - and this can happen through all levels of youth football.

If the FA wishes to improve the standards of the players in this country then they need to improve the quality of coaching. Educating young grassroots coaches in the ways that children actually develop and learn is being seen in the youth modules - which is positive. The new youth modules for football are much better than previous courses as they seek to educate coaches on *how* to coach and *how* children acquire skills and information instead of previous courses which taught *what* to coach. There is a big difference between having a session plan and a bag of balls and being *qualified* to work with children.

In reality there should not be anyone who works with a group of players who has not attended at least the Level 1 and 2 Youth Module awards. Too many volunteer coaches with a Level 1 award are regarded as coaches when, in truth, they are uneducated in the development of a young child, yet alone a young footballer.

The national playing style should be taught in the new FA youth modules and a five year target period should be applied to every coach to be working towards completion of the FA youth award (it involves attending the three youth module courses and carrying out a final assessment). More qualified coaches working under a national philosophy will be a positive step in developing more talented players.

With coaching such a critical component to success, we will need excellent coach educators. Unfortunately there are still cases of average and mediocre educators who neither inspire, educate, nor prepare coaches particularly well for their roles.

When considering quality coaching courses – they should not be viewed as 'buying the award' such that 'if you attend... you pass'. The assessment procedure from Level 1 upwards should be harder and more intense to make sure coaches put in the necessary work and commitment. Quantity is meaningless without quality.

Youth coaching should not be seen as a volunteer activity but an important and essential part of building the foundation of our next generation. The idea of coaching needs a culture change; it needs to be viewed as an occupation similar to that of a teacher not just a helpful volunteer. The FA needs to do a lot to address this issue yet 'we' (as coaches) also need to do something about it; we need to stop being apathetic to this crisis and stand up against poor standards which are ruining players in this country.

Finally, if the FA is serious about 'coach development' then they need to reduce the cost of their courses to make them accessible and affordable for many more grassroots coaches. Right now coach education courses are far too expensive and elitist and are restricting the development and understanding of many coaches.

> Football 'coaching' should no longer be seen as a 'volunteer' profession but as an important and respected part of youth development, for both football and social development.

# Solution 5 – Improve grassroots football

A coaching culture which values player development will see significant improvements and will increase the talent pool. The FA and county FAs need to monitor and support the grassroots game, as this is where the greatest number of players are.

The problem with 'dads' who help out is that they have no idea what they are doing. As mentioned above, a bag of balls and cones does not constitute a coach. I will make generalizations here which may be misplaced, as there are many good youth coaches out there, but there are many who use the same methods and thinking from when they were kids and how they were coached.

In turn, many methods are based on adult training and have no place or relevance for youth players. Fitness training for 8 year olds is something I have witnessed which has made me cringe and I worry that there are far more damaging coaches out there than good ones. These 'coaches' should not be working with young players, their intentions may be admirable but they are damaging the kids they work with. Every club should ultimately be a charter standard club where coaches are monitored and their qualifications are suited to their role. The FA has a major role to play in making sure the right people are working at this level.

The FA is introducing the FA mentor scheme yet they need to do much more to monitor coaching across the country. 50 coach mentors to work with grassroots clubs and coaches across the country is a positive step but still too small.

The culture right now is that academies are taking players at a young age to 'save' them from grassroots. However, a player should not have to be 'saved' from grassroots in order to receive a better education. Grassroots coaching should be better, it's as simple as that. High standards and the promotion of skill and creativity should be sought. The *win at all costs* mentality is ruining many players and destroying potential. Creativity is killed because it may lead to losing the ball. A change in the ethos for age groups 5-11 needs to happen so that much more emphasis is given to skill development and acquisition rather than results in matches.

It is also important to address the issue of relative age effect and for coaches to understand the differences in the early adolescent years when certain players are bigger or smaller depending on their date of birth. Perhaps splitting the grassroots into a six month age banding may help those players born May – August progress more than they do right now.

The grassroots game also needs a demarcation between participation and enjoyment, and more elite levels of grassroots. This way, players who wish to play football to simply enjoy it have the choice of community or elite. The *Midland Junior Premier League* is a good example of a higher standard of grassroots football that helps bridge the gap between grassroots and academy football.

There are several million children who enjoy playing and participating in football. They deserve a well organised, competitive, non-elitist and inclusive football environment. This environment can help players move up the levels of development.

> The grassroots game needs to be better managed
> and supported in order to give every player
> a positive experience - whatever their level.

# Solution 6 – Grassroots support coaches

If academies wish to have a larger pool of players to choose from then perhaps they need to do more to help the local grassroots clubs. If there was an elite level in the grassroots game then those coaches and players should receive more support from both the FA Skills programme and the local professional academy.

Imagine if both these organisations were helping coaches in the grassroots game. Standards and quality would certainly improve which would benefit players and ultimately give the academy a larger pool of talent to choose from. Therefore having a coach who works for the academy yet whose job is to support the local coaches of grassroots clubs would be something similar to the FA mentor scheme.

Academy coaches could carry out coach education and team training for local clubs. This could be the job of the foundation phase coach in academies who work with coaches for the Under-7 to Under-11 player levels.

Clubs should look beyond the first team and their immediate academy system and look at the wider picture. Professional academies should provide free coach education courses to local coaches which would also provide an opportunity for the club's philosophy to be embedded within a wider community framework.

If academies were restricted from using their pre-academies and instead went into local clubs to train players, then the issue of increased pressure and early specialisation would be limited. It would also help create a strong community bond which is lacking at this time (academies are often viewed negatively by locals).

In a nutshell, academies and Centres of Excellence need to give more back to the local clubs instead of just taking the talent; coach education clinics would be beneficial for grassroots coaches, showing them the drills and methods used within the Academy.

> Grassroots football needs to be supported by
> local academies that provide coach education
> and team training sessions.

# Solution 7 – FA led development centres

As well as academies needing to improve their own 'Development Centres', where it is often only Level 1 or 2 coaches who work with players, the FA needs to develop their own centres too. The key to both approaches being effective is to put in quality youth coaches who can improve the pool of talent.

The issue many academies face is that players coming in are often way off the level of their current players, even though the new players might excel in their grassroots environment. And when the academies release players they become guilty of allowing them to drop back to the bottom level where the quality of players and coaches is not as high. If the FA introduced elite development centres through their skills programme, then academies would have a more talented number of players moving up to their level. In turn, players released by academies would not be forced to move all the way back to grassroots but have a level which provides them with continued quality coaching.

A football framework should be structured which enables talented players to progress gradually whilst being continually challenged. The movement up from grassroots to academy lacks a middle area, where a skills programme should be. In

Germany, the centres support and further players with potential. Without this middle level, the pool of talent gets restricted and reduced.

It all comes down to cost, of course; the FA believes it is the job of academies to go into clubs and develop better coaches, and the academies believe it is the FA's role to push talent up. Ultimately it is the job of both parties. Once again, Germany's centres are a great example to follow. A lack of specialist coaches for younger age groups was addressed by the German FA who built 121 national talent centres in order to help 10 to 17-year-olds and who now employ more than 150 full-time coaches dedicated to working with younger children. These centres were supported by the talent development programme which was set up by the DFB in 2003 with the aim of identifying promising youngsters and providing them with technical skills and tactical knowledge at an early age.

Trevor Brooking initially looked to set up The FA skills programme to work with elite players, to improve their technical skills. The teaching of skills to master technique is precisely what has been missing from English youth development for decades. The English FA says it simply doesn't have the money to make this kind of investment.

What needs to happen is that the FA, working in conjunction with the Premier League, needs to fund the creation of development centres in order to 'bridge' the gap between grassroots and academies. If funding cannot be found from a £5 billion television deal then serious questions need to be asked.

> The implementation of development centres in every county across the country with selected gifted and talented players, working with expert coaches on weekly basis, will improve the quality of players and increase the talent pool.

# Solution 8 – Elitist academies

We have discussed the grassroots game and the importance of getting it right at this level - yet the money, facilities, and high quality coaching is in the academies, or more precisely in the Premier League clubs. When we talk of the best players, and of developing world class youth players, we are looking to the academies to make this happen. The truth right now is that academy football is a place which regards itself as elite yet which is most often an environment of mediocrity.

The new category system also needs to be implemented correctly. There are 26 Category One academies, but even this may be too many. If we wish to consider Category One as *the best* in England then it may be that we only need half this number to ensure that the top, elite academies are truly working with England's most talented players. Imagine if England had 10-12 of the finest academies working with the best talent, this would certainly help develop better players. It is Wilkinson's vision over 15 years later.

What cannot happen is for Category One academies to accept 'good' as a substitute for greatness. Category One needs to be the best, possessing the best coaches and philosophies which help develop players 'of the future'. These clubs should also have a clear pathway to the professional game and should be able to attract the most talented players in the country.

Academies need to become more elitist in their approach, methods and standards. They need to be world class environments for players to be pushed to the top levels of development and should not allow mediocrity.

Having higher quality coaches working with all age groups will enable younger age groups and more players to be exposed to better coaching. Of course, if academies want the best – they'll need to pay for the best. A full time member of staff for each age group is necessary. Candidly, professional football academies pay coaches a pittance compared to those who work in the senior game, let alone with professional players. This is wrong.

Many of England's talented coaches have left England to coach abroad. North America, Asia and the Middle East all pay coaches fortunes compared to what English academies do.

At the moment an academy coach can expect to earn around £15,000 to £22,000 a year. A full time coach in each age group with the necessary qualifications should be earning significantly more so that academies (fewer of them mind you; see above) attract and retain high calibre coaching talent. This is the elite level we are talking about. The time for low wages and mediocre personnel needs to change.

> The top academies need to become a place of elitism. World class coaches are essential; therefore world class working conditions and employment packages are necessary too.

# Solution 9 – Technical skills coaching

On top of increased investment in top class coaches every Category One academy should have a technical skills coach who works full time with the coaches, and players between the ages of 9 and 21.

In England, we develop athletes, putting too much faith in strength and speed and not enough on technical ability or intelligence. We restrict creativity and produce one dimensional players who are predictable and slow. Quite simply our players lack the key technical skills to cope with top level football. At this time there are only a limited number of English players with these abilities and this needs to change.

George Prost at Southampton, Rene Meulensteen at Manchester United, and Liam Brady at Arsenal are all examples of technical skills experts who have influenced the technical development of the players at their clubs. It is little surprise therefore that these academies have developed some of the brightest talent in recent years. Category One academies need to have similar types of coaches involved.

Academies should see the position of technical skills coach as necessary for players between 7 and 11, right through to the age of 21. You can never stop improving skill and the need to be a world class technician is essential in today's game.

> Our players need to be world class technicians – therefore
> a full time technical skills coach is needed in
> every Category One academy across the country.

# Solution 10 – Modernising talent identification

As discussed, issues with coaching at grassroots and academy level have affected the development of quality players. Yet a big issue has also been the scouting of players from grassroots to academy football. Too much emphasis on physicality and strength over technical quality and intelligence has resulted in a disappointingly limited number of players coming through the 'system'. Many changes need to be made at this level in order for more English players to become professional players.

Talent identification courses need to become more rigorous. A three hour course is not sufficient to become a qualified scout. England needs better. A more intense and modernised version of the course is needed to develop talented scouts who can 'see' the players with potential. Of course it is a difficult task to guarantee any future talent yet we have found that intelligence and personality are key aspects of success at future elite levels.

More knowledge and understanding about late developers should also be encouraged. Academies would be smart to set up two teams from Under-14 to Under-18 in order to cater for the late developers; that way they receive the same coaching but are not denied the chance to develop in a world class environment. Belgium has proven the value to this approach.

Academies need to seriously consider the standards of their scouting personnel. They need to avoid looking at the short term and failing to see a player's potential. Too many potential Xavis and Messis are being ignored and rejected due to their size and age. Many nations are starting to see that size is far less relevant than previously imagined. What is important is that players possess particular physical skills such as balance, agility and speed. Scouts need to pay greater attention to these attributes.

> The modern game requires intelligent, humble and hardworking players – therefore a greater understanding and appreciation for 'intelligence' and 'personality' should be what scouts and talent identification programmes focus on.

# Solution 11 – Improved sport science

The increase in contact time through the EPPP should be used to develop not just technical, but tactical, psychological and physical aspects too. A holistic approach to development should be implemented to develop fully rounded players.

There is much criticism of the English game for promoting physicality over skill leading to giants in youth football and the restriction of creative players. Yet the role of being a great athlete cannot be ignored. The future game will see a significant enhancement in the athletic capabilities of players and coaches should be aware of this and seek to enhance it with their players.

There will be increased physical demands in the future due to the speed of the game, a higher tempo of ball movement and faster opposition – this will mean speed, agility, and endurance will be paramount. As the ball is kept in play more and games are longer - players will cover greater distances. Greater distances and higher speeds mean more sprints at higher intensities. It is believed that players will need to cover between 12 and 15km in a match, at different speeds and directions. Therefore 'athleticism' is essential.

The ability to move with speed with the ball is also a key part of the game, and applies to all positions. The future game will require physical training to be position specific, and may even mean position specific coaches. The training of players who are capable of dealing with these demands will be essential.

Many academies are hiring sports scientists yet are not using them to their fullest potential. A few physical tests a year does not constitute developing a player's physical development and it appears that academies are often neglecting the importance of speed and agility development. Instead of measuring it and testing it they should be seeking to *develop* it in their players!

The sport scientists brought into academies should also be experts in bio-mechanics and the speed development which underpins elite development. Simply having a sports science degree is not enough. Staff need to be 'experts' in physical development *for football*.

> Academies need to be developing the speed and athleticism of their players and will require specialists to develop these key skills.

# Solution 12 – Introduction of sport psychologists

It is clear that sport psychology benefits many players and, it could be argued, what is between a player's ears is often the difference between becoming a professional or not.

With the pressures in academy environments coming from coaches and parents as well as the players themselves it is important that individuals are trained in controlling and developing their mindset, with a focus on producing players with the 'growth mindset'. Mindset has been proven to be one of the key elements for success. By neglecting the power and importance of the mind English football is failing many players.

Academies should look to engage full time sport psychologists who work with coaches, teams, and individuals in order to develop positive, 'growth' mindsets alongside improved performance through focus and concentration exercises. Coaches will benefit through improved communication and language skills and players will grow by focusing their minds on 'controllables'.

Perhaps a psychologist can help mould a player's approach to becoming a professional as far too many seem keen on wasting their careers when they reach 15-17 years of age. Psychological assistance can improve focus and the attitude to work harder, as well as being invaluable for those who 'lose their way'.

> The time for neglecting psychology is over – academies need to use sport psychology experts to enhance the development of players' minds and performance.

# Solution 13 – Summer season

Looking at the solutions mentioned so far at the grassroots level and in the academy set-up, then there is an underlying issue affecting all levels and ages of football across England: the weather.

There is no doubt that the climate in England has affected the development of more talented players. If we consider that the season runs from August – May then we have to be realistic and assume that players will only have roughly 12 weeks of 'good' weather in that season. The autumn and winter months bring bitterly cold temperatures which affect training and games in terms of cancellations, what can be practised, and more. As well as this, colder temperatures mean players need to be more 'active' which often results in high tempo games, a reflection of the English style.

Now imagine if the season was moved. It ran from February to November, and the winter months were regarded as the 'off-season'. Would this benefit the development of our players? Without question. There would be fewer cancellations and less time training in freezing cold and dark sessions. Football could be brighter and (slightly) warmer. This is not just for the players' enjoyment, this will allow more tactical development and teaching because coaches and players will be afforded environments which allow more rest, and temperatures which don't require full-on high tempo football in order to simply 'stay warm'.

The time off period (when cancellations occur most often) will benefit numerous groups, and for those who want to train during the 'off-season' then they can still hire pitches. Better still why not join a winter futsal league and have players develop their skills in a 'different' environment?

The greatest benefit of a move to a summer schedule is for academy players whom we wish to push to elite levels; they will be able to take greater advantage of the summer holidays. Too often the six week summer period is regarded as 'down time' for academies, yet this should be the time when the most activity, coaching and education is happening. Academies could have their players in for two or three full days a week, not just to play - but to learn in the classroom and work on their physical and mental development. The summer offers academies what they lack throughout the year: time.

One final benefit of playing in warmer temperatures would see our players 'learning' how to play in warm conditions. This may help address why we struggle in summer tournaments as we finally let our players play in summer months!

> Taking advantage of the time and weather which summer provides can be the answer for English players to compete with their foreign counterparts.

# Solution 14 – A greater bridge to senior football

If we improve the quality of young English players then perhaps more clubs will look to integrate them into the first team. Yet, right now, players between 16 and 21 are being lost too easily and the step up from youth to senior levels is not being addressed well enough. The introduction of the Under-21 league will enable players to stay in the 'youth development' environment for longer which should help late developers remain in the game. However it is important that players between 16 and 21 are given the chance to play and experience real senior competition.

Owners of Premier League clubs should be responsible for investing in the future not just the present. It must be required that anyone willing to invest in an English side has the intention to lay down plans and invest in infrastructure, facilities and high quality coaching in order to improve the long term development of English players and the sustainability of their clubs.

Right now English football is crippled by short-termism, a phenomenon where instant success is valued above long term sustainability. This leads to player acquisition on ludicrous contracts which consequently reduce the opportunities for younger players.

Clubs in the Premier League have twisted the 'home grown' ruling and allowed non-English players to be classed as 'home grown'. A squad of 25 requires eight 'home grown' players yet they do not need to be English players. This loophole is damaging and needs to be changed to mean English players only. Without question this will force clubs to push the development of their academy players.

Even better would be the introduction of FIFA's 6+5 rule which is used much more stringently in Germany. In Germany the 6+5 rule enables more players to gain the necessary experience to improve and take their skills from their youth education into the senior levels. If English youth sides were forced to use the 6+5 rule up to their Under-21 level then once again more English players would be given the opportunity and experience they require to develop.

Another solution might be a new rule which completely prevents foreign players being signed or bought until the age of 18. Alternatively, the Premier League should restrict the number of foreign players in youth squads and allow clubs only four per squad. This way a squad of 16-18 players will have 12-14 players who are English. There is no doubt this rule will aid their development. The worry is that political willpower will make these changes difficult to implement.

> Forcing clubs to concentrate on developing their own
> local talent, instead of casting the nets ever wider
> across the world, appears a necessity for getting
> more English players into the game.

# Solution 15 – Stricter international rules

The national team and the battle between club and country... There is clearly a lack of respect given to international youth tournaments. In the best interests of talented English players, the FA and clubs should continue to work together to support the production of talented English players for England teams but there needs to be greater enforcement of talented English players experiencing international football at age specific levels.

A key opportunity to gain experience and knowledge of international football is through tournaments. When there is a tournament, surely those who are eligible to play should represent their country? Yet we seem to have perennial issues of injury and unavailability. No wonder we struggle in tournaments, our young players are not used to them.

The worry for England has always been the neglect or even arrogance shown to these youth competitions, where many players (with clubs pulling the strings) will choose not to travel and represent their country. Many believe themselves to be too good for that level or prefer to preserve themselves for the more important season ahead for their clubs. This has led to a lack of experience and minimised the cohesion between players. Development and progression into the senior ranks is diminished.

When you look at Spain's success, their cohesiveness has come from development through the youth ranks of international football. Their recent success has been built on the education and experience of players gained through youth competitions. The bonds built, the knowledge gained at top level tournaments, and the relationships built between players, both on and off the pitch, have laid the foundation for the side we see today.

The FA must seek to make sure their youth sides are filled with the most talented players available. They need to be harder on clubs to make sure players attend matches when called up and they need to stop 'fast tracking' talented young players to the senior set up... where they often just sit on the bench.

One solution could be that selection for the national side (at whatever level) is non-negotiable. When selected, that player must attend the call. He must attend the team meeting, and the games, even if 'injured'. The clubs should not have control of whether the player goes or not. If 'injured' the player can still receive treatment from the medical staff of the national team. A failure to attend, or refusing a call-up, should result in serious sanctions. A ban, for example.

There should be no arguments about being selected for the national team and if players (or their clubs) do not wish to attend then they should be retired from international football. It should be this stringent.

> The FA needs to show more support for international youth
> tournaments by making sure the best team is assembled.
> They also need to be stronger about international call-ups
> and should not be dictated to by the clubs.

## Solution 16 – Moving abroad

We have spoken of the difficulties of breaking through to first teams, between the age of 17 and 21 in the Premier League, and how this can hamper the development of players. For some the only option is to go to the Championship and play there. This is not a bad thing yet what about more players exploring other options?

English players often display an unwillingness to take their career abroad. In the past decades there have been players such as Keegan, Platt, Gascoigne, Lineker, Waddle, Wilkins and Hoddle who have ventured to the continent in order to further their careers and learn new things. In the past fifteen years however there have only been a few top level players who have made the decision to move abroad: Ince, McManaman, Beckham and Owen are players who all moved abroad when in the prime of their careers. Paul Ince spoke recently about how moving to Italy furthered him as a player. He said it made him understand the game more and changed his approach to how he played it.

Is there a correlation between the lack of top quality English players moving abroad and England's lack of success in international football? Would some of England's better players have improved their game if they had moved to Italy, Spain or Germany? Would many of those young players, who are playing in youth sides and not getting their chance in the first team, benefit from playing abroad?

Why don't players move abroad and seek to learn new things; experience different cultures and new styles of play. Why should English players limit themselves to playing in England only? The game is becoming increasingly globalised. It will increase the number of English players playing and may actually enhance the quality of the talent pool.

> English players – both young and experienced – should
> look to move abroad in order to further their
> development, both as players and people.

# Solution 17 – Bringing everyone together

The final clear issue that needs to be addressed is one of cooperation. For English football to excel we will require the Premier League, professional clubs, the FA, and the Football League to all work together.

At the moment, internal politics between the FA, the Premier League and the Football League have repeatedly sabotaged attempts to bring about meaningful reform. Until the governing bodies in England agree that clubs must have more English players in their teams, and enforce a quota system, then the national team will not improve.

Too much fighting between these three organisations has resulted in poor management and planning that has restricted the development of a larger pool of talented players. There is a short-sightedness to the English development model which restricts the long term development of players.

Unfortunately the problem with the English league is that it talks a lot, and promises a brighter future, yet there is no governing body in total control of youth development. Just ask the Germans how cohesion and working together took their game forward.

> English football's future will take the combined effort of
> all bodies to achieve positive goals.

# A brighter future

As we near the end of this journey across England's past, present, and future, it is important that we realise that for too many years we have sat idly back waiting for change to happen. This kind of breath-holding or apathy cannot continue if we wish to see major change across our national game. It is important for us all to realise that real change takes a combined effort and that it is not just the FA or Premier League who hold the key to the future of English football. It is also coaches, parents and fans of the game. Our influence and impact can be just as important.

Ultimately the progression from grassroots football to the senior game is unpredictable and it is difficult to assume that any particular player can make it.

Thus, if we increase the pool of talent across the country and improve the quality of players who are capable of playing in the modern game, then we allow ourselves to have more English players in the Premier League and more options for the national team manager to select from.

Yes, it will take time and patience, but the current predicament is a broken one. What is key is that everyone works together to improve the levels and quality of players and coaching in the country, and that we take pride in doing our bit for the development of England's future.

Progression through the levels should be valued and promoted in order to push the best to the top. Elite should no longer be viewed as negative but as the aim of all coaches. We need to take satisfaction in our influence on the players' development pathway. And when England lifts the World Cup we can all be proud of the part we have played, whether small or large, in making the dream a reality.

# Bibliography

## Books

Abrahams, D. (2012). *Soccer Tough*. Bennion Kearny.

Bomba, T. & Haff, G. (2009). *Periodization: Theory and Methodology of Training 5th Edition*. Human Kinetics.

Coyle, D. (2009). *The Talent Code: Greatness Isn't Born. It's Grown. Here's How*. Bantam.

Doidge, N. (2007). *The brain that changes itself : Stories of Personal Triumph from the Frontiers of Brain Science*. Penguin.

Dweck, C. (2006). *Mindset*. Ballantine.

Gerrard, S. (2006). *Gerrard: My Autobiography*. Bantam Press.

Gladwell, M. (2008). *Outliers – The Story Of Success*. Penguin.

Green, C. (2009). *Every Boy's Dream*. A&L Black.

Howe, M. (2001). *Genius Explained*. Cambridge University Press.

Hughes, C. (1990). *The Winning Formula: Soccer Skills and Tactics*. HarperCollins.

Kormelink, H. & Seeverens, T. (1997). *The Coaching Philosophies of Louis van Gaal and the Ajax Coaches*. Reedswain.

Starkes, J. & Ericsson, K. (2003). *Expert Performance in Sports: Advances in Research on Sport Expertise*. Human Kinetics.

Syed, M. (2010). *Bounce – The Myth of Talent and Practice*. Fourth Estate.

Verheijen, R. (1998). *Conditioning for Soccer*. Reedswain.

Wagg, S. (2004). *British Football and Social Exclusion*. Routledge.

Wein, H. (2004). *Developing Game Intelligence in Soccer*. Reedwain.

Wein, H. (2007). *Developing Youth Football Players*. Human Kinetics.

**Bibliography**

Whitmore, J. (2002). *Coaching For Performance: Growing People, Performance and Purpose.* Nicholas Brealey.

Wilson, J. (2008). *Inverting the Pyramid – A History of Football Tactics.* Orion.

Winner, D. (2000). *Brilliant Orange – the neurotic genius of Dutch football.* Bloomsbury.

Zauli, A. (2002). *Soccer: Modern Tactics.* Reedswain.


## Online articles

Fifield, D. (2007). *'Golden generation' must take the blame for failure.* http://www.guardian.co.uk/football/2007/nov/23/newsstory.sport2

Collett, M. (2007.) *Croatia follow in Hungary's footsteps and give England a Wembley lesson.* http://blogs.reuters.com/soccer/2007/11/22/croatia-follow-in-hungarys-footsteps-and-give-england-a-wembley-lesson/

Austin, S. & Slater, M. (2008). *England player numbers at new low.* http://news.bbc.co.uk/sport2/hi/football/7417746.stm

Daily Mail. (2009). *England 2 Croatia 3: November 21, 2007...the date that still haunts English football.* http://www.dailymail.co.uk/sport/football/article-1212096/England-2-Croatia-3-November-21-2007--date-haunts-English-football.html

Morris, J. (2006.) *This was no English victory says Taylor.* http://www.guardian.co.uk/football/2006/mar/10/championsleague2

Professional Football Association. (2007). *Meltdown Report.* http://edition.pagesuite-professional.co.uk/launch.aspx?pnum=3&eid=095118a5-4201-40ae-a055-1a7e3cf16837

EPFL. *Home-grown quota for Premier League.* http://www.epfl-europeanleagues.com/quota_for_Premier_League.htm

Summerton, A. (2012). *English Football's Identity Crisis.* http://sabotagetimes.com/reportage/english-footballs-identity-crisis/

Wilson, J. (2012). *The Question: Does 4-4-2 work for England?* http://www.guardian.co.uk/sport/blog/2012/jun/05/euro-2012-roy-hodgson-england-tactics

Hoddle, G. (2012). *England need a tactical revolution.*
http://espnfc.com/euro2012/uk/en/features/1116745/glenn-hoddleengland-need-tactical-revolution.html

Hoddle, G. (2010). *What it's like to be the England boss at the World Cup.*
http://www.dailymail.co.uk/sport/worldcup2010/article-1282352/GLENN-HODDLE-What-like-England-boss-World-Cup.html

BBC Sport. (2012). *Rooney wins Wenger praise.*
http://news.bbc.co.uk/sport2/hi/football/eng_prem/2343809.stm

BBC Sport. (2010). *World Cup 2010: England talent worries me – Wilkinson.*
http://news.bbc.co.uk/sport1/hi/football/world_cup_2010/8770192.stm

Jensen, P. (2011). *Xavi: Paul Scholes is the best midfield player of the last 20 years.*
http://www.dailymail.co.uk/sport/football/article-1355726/Xavi-interview-Paul-Scholes-best-midfielder-20-years.html

Weaver, P. (2013). *Wilkinson frets over future of academies as clubs look elsewhere.*
http://www.guardian.co.uk/football/2007/nov/13/newsstory.sport1

Hill, J. (2010) *England's mistake was long forseen.*
http://www.expressandstar.com/sport/2010/07/01/an-england-analysis-ahead-of-its-time/

Gross, J. (2011). *The 'Elite Player Performance Plan' Will Kill Our Game.*
http://onthefutbol.wordpress.com/2011/10/23/the-elite-player-performance-plan-will-kill-our-game/

Roddy, G. (2011). *Elite Player Performance Plan will put youngsters on a par with continental contemporaries.* http://www.telegraph.co.uk/sport/football/competitions/premier-league/8956990/Elite-Player-Performance-Plan-will-put-youngsters-on-a-par-with-continental-contemporaries-says-Ged-Roddy-Premier-League-Youth-Director.html

The Scratching Head. (2011). *The EPPP: Is It Really Such A Bad Thing?*
http://www.thescratchingshed.com/2011/10/the-eppp-is-it-really-such-a-bad-thing/

Fustalfutbol. (2012). *EPPP or Futsal – Why are England so resistant?* http://futsal-futbol.com/futsal-ramble/eppp-or-futsal/

Bowler, D. (2012). *Only the Best Will Do?*
http://www.firsttouchonline.com/2012/03/only-the-best-will-do/

# Bibliography

Jordan, S. (2011). *Carry on cherry-picking: field day for Premier League talent poachers.* http://www.guardian.co.uk/football/blog/2011/nov/03/premier-league-football-league-academy

Fletcher, P. (2011). *Youth overhaul will damage Football League.* http://www.bbc.co.uk/blogs/paulfletcher/2011/10/football_league_votes_in_favou.html

Bevan, D. (2011). *Why do Crystal Palace and Watford disagree on EPPP?* http://thetwounfortunates.com/why-do-crystal-palace-and-watford-disagree-on-eppp/

Winter, H. (2011). *Premier League's elite plan radical overhaul of academy system to help top schoolboy talent.* http://www.telegraph.co.uk/sport/football/competitions/premier-league/8324495/Henry-Winter-Premier-Leagues-elite-plan-radical-overhaul-of-academy-system-to-help-top-schoolboy-talent.html

Donnelly, L. (2011). *Children 'getting weaker because they don't climb trees'.* http://www.telegraph.co.uk/health/children_shealth/8528464/Children-getting-weaker-because-they-dont-climb-trees.html

The Perfect Hattrick. (2013.) *The rise of futsal and its influence on football.* http://www.perfecthattrick.co.uk/?p=175

Rizvi, A. (2012). *Futsal is football with fast-forward button.* http://www.thenational.ae/sport/football/futsal-is-football-with-fast-forward-button-pressed

Escolla Futsal. (2013). *What is Futsal?* http://www.escollafutsal.com/index.php/what-we-do

Deacon, A. (2013). *Futsal is the key to England ending the years of hurt.* http://backpagefootball.com/futsal-is-the-key-to-england-ending-the-years-of-hurt/53493/

Winter, H. (2007). *FA insist Manchester United show way forward.* http://www.telegraph.co.uk/sport/football/teams/england/2328951/FA-insist-Manchester-United-show-way-forward.html

Boyle, M. (2013). *Early Specialization in Sports.* http://www.agilitydoctor.com/learning/agility-magazine/218-early-specialization-in-sports

De Lench, B. (2012). *Delay Sport Specialization Until Late Adolescence, Experts Say.* http://www.momsteam.com/successful-parenting/delay-sport-specialization-until-late-adolescence-experts-say

De Lench, B. (2012). *Early Sports Specialization Can Interfere With Healthy Child Development, Lead to Social Isolation.* http://www.momsteam.com/successful-parenting/early-sport-specialization-may-interfere-with-healthy-child-development-increase-social-isolation

Duncan, C. (2011). *Early Specialisation – Seeing the Big Picture.* http://www.drcraigduncan.com/2011/09/14/early-specialisation-seeing-the-big-picture/

De Lench, B. (2012). *Preventing Overuse Injuries in Youth Athletes.* http://www.momsteam.com/overuse/preventing-overuse-injuries-in-youth-athletes

De Lench, B. (2012). *Overuse Injury Epidemic Result Of Year-Round Play, Too Many Teams At Same Time.* http://www.momsteam.com/successful-parenting/-overuse-injury-epidemic-result-year-round-play-too-many-teams-at-same-time

Richardson, H. (2013). *'Not enough strenuous activity' in school PE.* http://www.bbc.co.uk/news/education-21449610

Helm, T. & Asthana, A. (2010). *Michael Gove's plan to slash sports funding in schools splits cabinet.* http://www.guardian.co.uk/education/2010/nov/20/michael-gove-schools-sport-funding

The Guardian. (2010). *Olympians protest over 'mind-blowing' cuts to school sport funding.* http://www.guardian.co.uk/sport/2010/oct/27/olympic-athletes-cuts-school-sport

Magowan, A. (2010). *The real state of English coaching.* http://news.bbc.co.uk/sport2/hi/football/8785895.stm

Weaver, P. (2007). *Wilkinson frets over future of academies as clubs look elsewhere.* http://www.guardian.co.uk/football/2007/nov/13/newsstory.sport1

Walker, M. (2011). *The fight to stop England's international talent pool running dry.* http://www.dailymail.co.uk/sport/football/article-2074231/Englands-future-international-talent-running-dry.html

Williams, S. (2009). *Football academies: kicking and screaming.* http://www.telegraph.co.uk/sport/football/4938593/Football-academies-kicking-and-screaming.html

# Bibliography

Football Australia. (2012). *De Boer backs Ajax philosophy.*
http://www.footballaustralia.com.au/world/news-display/de-boer-backs-ajax-philosophy/52861

Draper, R. (2011). *Cruyff: All great teams have home-grown players... otherwise they end up like City and Tevez.* http://www.dailymail.co.uk/sport/football/article-2049600/Cruyff-All-great-teams-home-grown-players--end-like-City-Tevez.html

Hill, A. (2013). *Young footballers show signs of burnout.*
http://www.leeds.ac.uk/news/article/3364/young_footballers_show_signs_of_burnout

Barlow, M. (2007). *Academies of lost youth: System is failing our youngsters, says Wilko.*
http://www.dailymail.co.uk/sport/football/article-436520/Academies-lost-youth-System-failing-youngsters-says-Wilko.html

Harris, N. (2011). *After Walcott, Bale and Oxlade-Chamberlain, Southampton are aiming to create a new golden generation for England.*
http://www.dailymail.co.uk/sport/football/article-2060821/After-Walcott-Bale-Oxlade-Chamberlain-Southampton-aiming-create-new-golden-generation-England.html

Field, D. (2011). *Alex Oxlade-Chamberlain is another Southampton academy success story.*
http://www.guardian.co.uk/football/blog/2011/jan/28/southampton-alex-oxlade-chamberlain

Grech, P. (2013). *In Search of Game Intelligence.*
http://www.blueprintforfootball.com/2013/04/in-search-of-game-intelligence.html

Sinnott, J. (2011). *Standard Liege's Bruyninckx leads way in developing mental capacity.*
http://sportsillustrated.cnn.com/2011/soccer/12/17/blizzard.sinnott.mental/index.html

Peterson, D. (2012). *Sports Are 80 Percent Mental Michel Bruyninckx Trains Soccer Brains.*
http://blog.80percentmental.com/2012/01/michel-bruyninckx-trains-soccer-brains.html

Sinnott, J. (2011). *Cracking coaching's final frontier*
.http://news.bbc.co.uk/sport2/hi/football/9421702.stm

Peterson, D. (2012). *Teaching your brain how to play soccer.*
http://www.axonpotential.com/teaching-your-brain-how-to-play-soccer/

Scott, M. (2010). *Football coach shortage paints bleak picture for England's future.*
http://www.guardian.co.uk/football/2010/jun/01/football-coach-shortage-england

James, S. (2012). *Steve McClaren: young players in Holland are much more advanced.*
http://www.guardian.co.uk/football/2012/dec/22/steve-mcclaren-coaching-the-coaches

Sheringham, S. (2010). Liverpool coach Borrell says academy 'was unacceptable'.
http://news.bbc.co.uk/sport2/hi/football/teams/l/liverpool/8611991.stm

Chelseafc.com. (2013). *Nextgen: Drummy expects final to entertain.*
http://www.chelseafc.com/news-article/article/3126309

Law, M. (2013).*Youth of today: Chelsea must give superkids a proper chance, urges youth coach.*
http://www.mirror.co.uk/sport/football/news/chelsea-must-give-superkids-proper-1794398

Clavane, A. & Sammers, S. (2013). *'The money never motivated me': John Bostock reflects on a career that has taken him from Tottenham to Toronto.*
http://www.mirror.co.uk/sport/football/news/john-bostock-reflects-career-taken-1794125

Walker, M. (2011). *I was let down, says former Chelsea starlet Taiwo.*
http://www.dailymail.co.uk/sport/football/article-2051541/Former-Chelsea-starlet-Taiwo-I-let-down.html

Ronay, B. (2011). *Homespun philosophy of Crewe's Dario Gradi recognised by Football League.*
http://www.guardian.co.uk/football/football-league-blog/2011/mar/21/dario-gradi-crewe-football-league-crewe

Tribal Football. (2011). *FC Twente frustrated over agents claims for Man City striker Guidetti.* http://www.tribalfootball.com/articles/fc-twente-frustrated-over-agents-claims-man-city-striker-guidetti-1699351

Benitez, R. (2012). *Quo Vadis EPL?*
http://www.rafabenitez.com/web/index.php?act=mostrarBlog&id_entrada=109&pag=7&idioma=in

Jackson, J. (2010). *Germany provide the blueprint for England's academy system.*
http://www.guardian.co.uk/football/2010/jul/04/germany-youth-development-england

## Bibliography

Oakley, B. (2012). *How to build a champion: Be born at the right time.*
http://www.bbc.co.uk/sport/0/olympics/18891749

Jackson, J. (2011). *FA plans change for young talent to overcome the relative age effect.*
http://www.guardian.co.uk/football/2011/jun/19/fa-plans-age-group-football

Glynn, P. (2011). *Other shores : Belgium* The FA Bootroom [Issue 1].
http://fa.edocs.co.uk/ebooks/boot_room/index.html#/44/

Glynn, P. (2009). *Stop throwing mud.* The FA.com Get Into Football.
http://www.thefa.com/GetIntoFootball/Coaches/FATescoSkillsColumn/Stop_thr
owing_mud

FourFourTwo. (2013). *Lilleshall – Football's answer to Hogwarts.*
http://fourfourtwo.com/blogs/fourfourtwoview/archive/2013/02/05/in-the-new-
issue-inside-borussia-dortmund-gerrard-amp-carra-in-conversation.aspx

Jagger, C. (2012). *Talent Identification: Football Club Player Scouting.* http://www.spain-
football.culturespain.com/2012/09/talent-identification-football-club-player-
scouting/

Keassel, A. (2009). *Theo Walcott: the making of a prodigy.*
http://www.guardian.co.uk/football/2009/sep/20/theo-walcott-interview-arsenal

Winter, H. (2012). *Spain's magical team show just how far behind England have fallen in the
international game.*
http://www.telegraph.co.uk/sport/football/teams/england/9371138/Spains-
magical-team-show-just-how-far-behind-England-have-fallen-in-the-international-
game.html

Beane, T. (2013). *Johan Cruyff on Youth Development.*
http://www.cruyfffootball.com/uncategorized/blog-post-one/

Leonard, K. (2010). *Huge acclaim for 'grounded' Gareth Bale.*
http://www.bbc.co.uk/news/mobile/uk-wales-11684062

Breeze, J. (2011). *'Alex Oxlade-Chamberlain is a real talent' - Stuart Pearce hails Arsenal
youngster after England under-21 hat-trick.* http://www.goal.com/en-
gb/news/2896/premier-league/2011/10/07/2700629/alex-oxlade-chamberlain-is-
a-real-talent-stuart-pearce-hails

*Michael Jordan - Cut From His High School Team.*
http://sports.jrank.org/pages/2387/Jordan-Michael-Cut-from-His-High-School-Team.html

Saffer, P. (2009). *Sammer talks up German youth talent.*
http://www.uefa.com/news/newsid=821592.html

James, S. (2013). *How Germany went from bust to boom on the talent production line.*
http://www.guardian.co.uk/football/2013/may/23/germany-bust-boom-talent

Hermanns, S. & Rosentritt, M. (2013). *"Dann läuft der Titel auf uns zu".*
http://www.tagesspiegel.de/sport/dfb-sportdirektor-robin-dutt-dann-laeuft-der-titel-auf-uns-zu/8191914.html

Dobson, T. (2010). *Fan-based ownership a solution for A-League?*
http://www.greenleft.org.au/node/46190

Bond, D. (2013). *Has the evolution of the beautiful game been for better or worse?*
http://www.bbc.co.uk/sport/0/football/22314015

BBC Sport. (2013). *FA's Dyke wants more English youngsters in Premier League.*
http://www.bbc.co.uk/sport/0/football/22680882

Gibson, O. (2013). *English football 'has a year to change' say MPs preparing to urge legislation.*
http://www.guardian.co.uk/football/2013/jan/29/english-football-mps-threaten-reform

Edwards, J. (2013). *New FA chairman Dyke says big-money Premier League damages England chances.* http://www.dailymail.co.uk/sport/football/article-2331696/Greg-Dyke-says-Premier-League-harming-England-team.html

Roan, D. (2011). *The Numbers Game - FA facing participation challenge.*
http://www.bbc.co.uk/blogs/danroan/2011/06/tough_times_for_grassroots_foo.html

Club website. (2012). *FA proposals for youth football – one step to go.*
http://www.clubwebsite.co.uk/news/2012/04/27/fa-proposals-for-youth-football-one-step-to-go/

# Journals

Ericsson, A. (2004). Deliberate Practice and the Acquisition and Maintenance of Expert Performance in Medicine and Related Domains. *Academic Medicine*, 79 (10), pp S70-S81.

Franzen, J., Pion, J., Vandendriessche, J., Vandorpe, B., Vaeyens, R., Lenior, M. & Philippaerts, R. (2012). Differences in physical fitness and gross motor coordination in boys aged 6-12 years specializing in one versus sampling more than one sport. *Journal of Sports Sciences*, 30 (4), 379-386.

Helsen, W., van Winckel, J. & Williams, A. (2005). The relative age effect in youth soccer across Europe. *Journal of Sports Sciences*, 23 (6), 629-636.

Lenroot, R.K. & Giedd, J.N. (2006). Brain development in children and adolescents: Insights from anatomical magnetic resonance imaging. *Neuroscience and Biobehavioral Reviews*, 30. 718–729.

MacNamara , A., Button, A., & Collins, D. (2010). The Role of Psychological Characteristics in Facilitating the Pathway to Elite Performance Part 1: Identifying Mental Skills and Behaviors. *The Sport Psychologist*, 24, 52-73.

Mehrabian, A., & Wiener, M. (1967). Decoding of Inconsistent Communications. *Journal of Personality and Social Psychology*, 6(1), 109–114.

Vaeyens, R., Mujika, I., Matthys, S., Santisteban, J., Goiriena, J. & Philippaerts, R. (2009). The relative age effect in a professional football club setting. *Journal of Sports Sciences*, 27 (11), 1153-1158.

Vaeyens, R., Güllichb, A., Warrc, C. & Philippaerts, R. (2009). Talent identification and promotion programmes of Olympic athletes. *Journal of Sports Sciences*, 27 (13), 1367-1380.

Vaeyens, R., Lenoir, M., Williams, A. & Philippaerts, R. (2008). Talent identification and development programmes in sport: current models and future directions. *Sports Medicine*, 38 (9), 703-714.

Ward, P., Hodges, N., Starkes, J. & Williams, M. (2007). The road to excellence: deliberate practice and the development of expertise. *High Ability Studies*, 18 (2), 119-153.

Williams, A.M. & Hodge, N.J. (2005). Practice, Instruction and skill acquisition on soccer: challenging tradition. *Journal of Sports Science.* 23 (6), 637-50.


# Presentations

Belgian youth development
http://www.nzs.si/resources/files/doc/dokumenti/ostali_dokumenti/Mladinski_n apredek_Belgija.pdf

Duncan, M. (2011) *Talent Identification.* Coventry University
http://www.scienceandfootball.com/Uploads/306.pdf

## Graduation: Life Lessons of a Professional Footballer by Richard Lee

The 2010/11 season will go down as a memorable one for Goalkeeper Richard Lee. Cup wins, penalty saves, hypnotherapy and injury would follow, but these things only tell a small part of the tale. Filled with anecdotes, insights, humour and honesty - Graduation uncovers Richard's campaign to take back the number one spot, save a lot of penalties, and overcome new challenges. What we see is a transformation - beautifully encapsulated in this extraordinary season.

*"Whatever level you have played the beautiful game and whether a goalkeeper or outfield player, you will connect with this book. Richard's honesty exposes the fragility in us all, he gives an honest insight into dimensions of a footballer's life that are often kept a secret and in doing so offers worthy advice on how to overcome any hurdle. A great read."* **Ben Foster, Goalkeeper, West Bromwich Albion.**

## Soccer Tough by Dan Abrahams

"Take a minute to slip into the mind of one of the world's greatest soccer players and imagine a stadium around you. Picture a performance under the lights and mentally play the perfect game."

Technique, speed and tactical execution are crucial components of winning soccer, but it is mental toughness that marks out the very best players – the ability to play when pressure is highest, the opposition is strongest, and fear is greatest. Top players and coaches understand the importance of sport psychology in soccer but how do you actually train your mind to become the best player you can be?

Soccer Tough demystifies this crucial side of the game and offers practical techniques that will enable soccer players of all abilities to actively develop focus, energy, and confidence. Soccer Tough will help banish the fear, mistakes, and mental limits that holds players back.

## Scientific Approaches to Goalkeeping in Football: A practical perspective on the most unique position in sport
by Andy Elleray

Do you coach goalkeepers and want to help them realise their fullest potential? Are you a goalkeeper looking to reach the top of your game? Then search no further and dive into this dedicated goalkeeping resource. Written by goalkeeping guru Andy Elleray this book offers a fresh and innovative approach to goalkeeping in football. With a particular emphasis on the development of young goalkeepers, it sheds light on training, player development, match performances, and player analysis. Utilising his own experiences Andy shows the reader various approaches, systems and exercises that will enable goalkeepers to train effectively and appropriately to bring out the very best in them.

## Small Time: A Life in the Football Wilderness by Justin Bryant

In 1988, 23-year-old American goalkeeper Justin Bryant thought a glorious career in professional football awaited him. He had just saved two penalties for his American club - the Orlando Lions - against Scotland's Dunfermline Athletic, to help claim the first piece of silverware in their history. He was young, strong, healthy, and confident.

Small Time is the story of a life spent mostly in the backwaters of the game. As Justin negotiated the Non-League pitches of the Vauxhall-Opel League, and the many failed professional leagues of the U.S. in the 1980s and 90s - Football, he learned, is 95% blood, sweat, and tears; but if you love it enough, the other 5% makes up for it.

## Soccer Brain: The 4C Coaching Model for Developing World Class Player Mindsets and a Winning Football Team
by Dan Abrahams

Coaching soccer is demanding. Impossible to perfect, it requires a broad knowledge of many performance areas including technique, tactics, psychology and the social aspects of human development. The first two components are covered in detail in many texts – but Soccer Brain uniquely offers a comprehensive guide to developing the latter two – player mindsets and winning teams.

Soccer Brain is for the no limits coach. It's for the coach who is passionate about developing players and building a winning team. This is not a traditional soccer coaching book filled with drills or tactics or playing patterns. This book is about getting the very best from you, the coach, and helping you develop a coaching culture of excellence and world class football mindsets.

## Saturday Afternoon Fever: A Year On The Road For Soccer Saturday
by Johnny Phillips

You might already know Johnny Phillips. He is a football reporter for Sky Sports' Soccer Saturday programme and a man who gets beamed into the homes of fans across the country every weekend.

For the 2012/13 season, Johnny decided to do something different. He wanted to look beneath the veneer of household-name superstars and back-page glamour to chronicle a different side to our national sport. As Johnny travelled the country, he found a game that he loved even more, where the unheralded stars were not only driven by a desire to succeed but also told stories of bravery and overcoming adversity, often to be plucked from obscurity into the spotlight… and sometimes dropped back into obscurity again. Football stories that rarely see the limelight but have a value all fans can readily identify with.

Lightning Source UK Ltd.
Milton Keynes UK
UKOW06f0739180813

215517UK00007B/171/P